Guru Leela
Volume 4

Mohanji and I

Thanaletchmy Sridhar
Mohanji UK

Guru Leela
Volume 4
Mohanji and I

This book is a **Mohanji Satcharita** —
a collection of honest testimonials from
Mohanji's followers across the world

Ⓖ Gurulight

with Love
Mohanji

Guru Leela – Volume 4
Mohanji and I

Copyright 2021 Gurulight
All Rights Reserved

No part of this book may be reproduced,
or stored in a retrieval system,
or transmitted by
any means without the
written permission of the author.

ISBN No.: 978-81-935309-8-6

Acknowledgments & Credits

Cover Design: Mohana Hanumatananda

Cover Art: Andrijana Ristovska

Transcription, Editing & Proof Reading:
Rekha Murali, Shyama Jeyaseelan

Publication Coordination:
Subhasree Thottungal

First Edition published by GuruLight, 2021
Email: info@gurulight.com
Web: www.gurulight.com

A Friend Whom You Can Trust

We dedicate this book, 'Guru Leela Volume 4 – Mohanji & I' to our spiritual guide and eternal friend Mohanji, with immense gratitude and love. May these true and life-transforming testimonials inspire and elevate all those who read this book.

CONTENTS

From The Editors' Pen i

Foreword ix

My Tryst With Destiny 1
Ananth Nalabanda, UK

The Dimensions Of Mohanji 17
Ndifon Charles Londi, Canada

The Guru Who Liberates 29
Devadas, India

Witnessing The Grand Tradition 37
Elham Khordadian, USA

Faith 53
Eric Elbers, Canada

Path Of Pathlessness 65
Hein Adamson, South Africa

Guru Shikhar 77
Jayashree Mukund Shinde, USA

Calm Amidst The Storm 91
Madhusudan Rajagopalan, India

Resurrection Of Lazarus 105
A Mohanji Follower

Mastering Crises .... *Mohanji's Shadow*	111
Master's Grace In Kailash .... *Nikita Naredi, India*	123
The Art Of Forgiving.. *Rekha Murali, India*	137
A Life Of Purpose .... *Restituto Oqeundo, Philippines*	145
Love Transforms .... *Rowena Conlu, Philippines*	151
Faith And Fearlessness... *Shyama Jeyaseelan, UK*	157
Compassion Unlimited... *Subhasree Thottungal, UK*	177
Freedom From Patterns .... *Trent Leighton, Canada*	189
A Devotee Speaks... *Vasantha Bhavraju (Tayiji), India*	193
Goodnight Papa Mohanji.. *Bavani Anop, New Zealand*	207
Guru's Gifts .... *Biljana Vozarevic, Serbia*	211
I Think Mohanji Is Secretly My PA .... *George Obeng-Duro, USA*	215

The Man I Know Of 219
Preethi Gopalarathnam, India

Gratitude 223
Ulla Bernholdt, Denmark

Glossary 224

Disclaimer:

"The views, opinions and positions expressed by the authors on these testimonials are theirs alone, and do not necessarily reflect the views, opinions or positions of Mohanji, Mohanji Foundation, its members, employees or any other individual or entity associated with Mohanji or Mohanji Foundation. We make no representations as to accuracy, completeness, timeliness, suitability or validity of any information presented by individual authors and will not be liable for any errors, omissions, or delays in this information or any losses, injuries or damages arising from its display or use."

Gurulight

FROM THE EDITORS' PEN

It has been two years since the 1st volume of Guru Leela came into existence bringing the pearls of experiences with Mohanji. Thinking back, it seems like a dream how the idea was born, how Mohanji's grace and blessings helped the three of us to make this a reality, walking through this journey of Guru Leela series from volume 1 to volume 3.

Starting with the scanning of almost 500 testimonials that were already published by then, compiling, editing, and proofreading, it felt as though we were living through all those experiences ourselves! Compilation of Guru Leela is not just an editing job, and not any ordinary book publishing task. Every moment of this journey is a huge transformation for ourselves too - awareness, acceptance, surrender, faith and ultimate conviction.

Here we are again, very humbly presenting to you the 4th Volume of Guru Leela – "Mohanji & I".

The words 'Guru Leela' mean the divine play of the Guru (one's spiritual Master). This book series is about the spiritual Master and his *leelas*, his divine play, as experienced by his followers. These are honest testimonials that reveal the unshakable faith, uncompromising consistency and steadfast conviction of spiritual seekers globally.

Mohanji has said,

> "A true Guru gives experiences.
> He may not need words to deliver.
> Through silence, through a look
> or glance, he can light the fire of
> awareness in a true disciple, who is
> fully ripe and ready for liberation."

"Mohanji & I" is a colourful palette of the various hues of the Guru's grace, protection, and healing, through experiences in both tangible and intangible ways. Where there are faith and surrender, the follower never leaves empty-handed. The Guru always gives unconditionally, even if one is not aware of the blessings received.

The core of "Mohanji & I" is the deep connection of every follower with Mohanji. Every experience culminates in fulfilment of desires enabling the seeker to walk the path of liberation. It takes the follower closer to the Guru on the outside who guides us to the divinity within.

As we have seen through the numerous testimonials shared by the followers, the unique connection that each follower has established with Mohanji, the relationship with the eternal Master also becomes

From The Editors' Pen

unique, incomparable, uncompromised and most beautiful. For some, he is the rock-solid father; for some, the most compassionate, warm mother; for others, he is the perfect guide, the best buddy for many, and the eternal lover with divine romance for many more! For most, he is a combination of all these and is simply 'MOHANJI'. Whatever the shade is, HE IS ALWAYS THERE with each and every one! *"Main hoon na"* – meaning "I am there for you", are the words that Mohanji says most casually yet with the assurance and truth that brings 100% conviction for the follower. All you need to know is that Mohanji is not separate from you, Mohanji is not outside of you, Mohanji is not far from you. Mohanji is right inside you, Mohanji is with you. Mohanji is YOU!

In every story and poem that you will read in this volume of Guru Leela – "Mohanji & I", you will see exactly this. We can't compare, judge or measure these stories, nor do we need any evidence to prove their authenticity!

We respect the sincerity and truth in each writer's feelings in expressing their story in their words, in their style, and in their authentic way. While compiling these stories, we were taken aback by the variety in which each one has experienced different dimensions of Mohanji. Our logical mind cannot simply comprehend these. The only thing we could do was surrender and accept each of these expressions as flowers of love, devotion, faith and gratitude offered at the lotus feet of the Master. Then how can we judge criticise or reject these? We realised many stories were way above our analysing mind matter. Then we closed our eyes, listened to our heartbeat, and we could feel the essence, the honesty, the purity and the purest love.

That's exactly what we would recommend to each one of you, dear readers. When your mind creates doubt or resistance, simply surrender, look inside your heart, and you can feel the fragrance filling the air! Try it.

"Mohanji & I" is special because of these sincere offerings of love from Mohanji's followers. Our immense gratitude to the authors for being a source of inspiration to help our future generations understand our eternal guide, protector and friend, Mohanji.

We hope all the readers feel the power of Mohanji's divine *leelas* and his grace while reading these stories.

After reading this book, please send your feedback to 'testimonials@mohanji.org.'

We extend our sincere gratitude to K. D. Row for his honest sharing in the foreword about Mohanji.

From The Editors' Pen

Our sincere thanks to all the artists for their deep love for Mohanji, which can be witnessed through their sketches and paintings.

Our deepest appreciation to the book presentation team.

We share a few words on the heart-melting painting on the cover page. This is a sketch of a photo of Mohanji with Pravin Thakkar from London, taken during his Kailash pilgrimage in 2019. When we were thinking of how to show the uniqueness of "Mohanji &I", from many options that we scanned through, this picture just touched our hearts immediately. The three of us literally shouted out, "Yes! This is the one".

We reached out to our dear friend and a close follower of Mohanji, an extremely talented painter by profession, Andrijana Ristovska for the sketching. The love and warmth behind this photo couldn't be hidden from the eyes of the artist! She was excited to do it – "Anything for Guruji!" We then came to know that at that time, Andrijana was eight months pregnant! We hesitated a little not wanting to trouble her, especially since we didn't have a huge amount of time to complete the book. But Andrijana didn't hesitate even for a moment; she took this up so excitedly and kept updating us as the painting progressed. Within four weeks, the painting was in our mailbox! Our jaws dropped!

We couldn't keep this with ourselves; we had to show it to Mohanji! After all, it was Mohanji who made it happen! Mohanji appreciated the beauty, the attention to details and moreover the love with which it was done. Not just appreciation, Mohanji said something that made us realise, how practical and how truly appreciative Mohanji is, he always respects and appreciates! Mohanji said, "This painting (the original one) must be auctioned, and Andrijana must be rewarded for this." He truly valued this, beyond what we could have even thought of!

That's how Mohanji is. He never takes anything for granted, never demands anything, and never underestimates anything. When we see the humility with which he respects and appreciates the work and effort of people serving the mission, our heads bow down. A lot to learn from the simplicity of this extraordinary Master who is walking with us!

Coming back to the cover page design, we offer our loving gratitude to our dear brother Mohana Hanumatananda who has been designing every cover page for Guru Leela. Designing is not the only skill he has; he answers tons of our naïve questions, dealing with our rushed demands with his level headed coolness. He is the coolest brother in our Mohanji family, for sure.

How can we not mention Rajesh Kamath! The one and only Rajesh Kamath! (Well, you haven't

From The Editors' Pen

forgotten 'Miraculous Days with Mohanji (MWDM)' book, have you?) We thank our comrade Rajesh for his funny way of picking on us, but truly that was what we needed, the right guidance at the right time, bringing in just the right things! Thank you, Rajesh. We love you for what you are – Mohanji's dear 'Buddhu'.

Thank you James Subramaniam for the book layout and our dear Sarathy Mama for the printing! His advice on printing has been the backbone in getting Guru Leela into the form that you see now - easy to read, easy to carry, and uncompromised quality. After all, this is no ordinary book; this is **Mohanji Satcharita**, which will shine like the guiding star to many generations!

With deep love and respect, we thank you Mohanji for being our inspiration and strength, guiding us every step of the way towards making this book a reality. Our heartfelt gratitude to you for walking with us to eternity.

With love,

Rekha Murali, India
Shyama Jeyaseelan, London
Subhasree Thottungal, London
February 2021

Mohanji & K D Row

FOREWORD

A connection through lifetimes

Mr K D Row, a retired top executive of Air India and the Goa Public Service Commission's ex-chairman is an advisor to the Mohanji Foundation. While leading a successful career, Mr Row was also progressing on his spiritual journey when he met Mohanji a few years ago. Let us read on to find out more about the discovery and connection of his Guru in this lifetime.

Dear Gentle Reader,

The greatest miracle is that of human life! We have reached this stage of evolution after great effort and many lives before. The human being alone can discriminate between right and wrong, good and bad. The finest quality of compassion is bequeathed to him only on this planet.

Having these unique qualities, what more is there to be done? All other creatures eat, drink, procreate and die. Our innate, higher qualities have marked us for a higher purpose. This purpose is the quest - who am I? Am I just the body with its limited identity? Or am I something more? Over centuries, man has pondered over this and realised that some greater power set up, organised and operated this diverse universe. Who is this power? Can I know him? Something tells the mind and heart that there is a link, a channel, a path, a connection with that power!

In my life, this link or connection, call it what you may, appeared in the form of Mohanji.

It is said when the disciple is ready, the *Guru* appears! In my case, the Guru appeared literally in my house. I received a phone call one day, out of the blue, from a friend in Delhi. She wanted me to speak to someone. No reason was given. This person did not want anything, just wanted to say 'Hello'. Quite mystified, I agreed. That is when Mohanji come on the line, and his warm voice engulfed me. We exchanged courtesies, and I invited Mohanji to Goa. He readily agreed and said he would come, one day. Little did I know that a new chapter of my life had begun - the most important one.

A few months later, I received a call from Mohanji that he would like to visit Goa and have a *Satsang* here. I readily agreed. That was when I was introduced to a charming, ever-smiling young man, Madhusudan, who coordinated the visit. I was connected to another young man, Rajesh Kamath, who accompanied Mohanji on this visit. All the pieces were slowly falling into place, unknown to me.

Foreword

Mohanji's flight was later in the evening. I reached the airport, and for the first time, beheld Mohanji. I took his hands in mine, touched it to my forehead, and an electric current passed through me. I knew I had found my *Guru*! Words cannot express how amazing and out of the blue, this arrangement was by the divine.

At home, my wife was eagerly awaiting Mohanji. We performed *Pada Puja* and joyfully welcomed him. Our home was sanctified and purified by his presence. His utter simplicity, graciousness and magnetic smile bowled us over. My wife knew, just like me, that we had found our *Guru*.

The next four days were spent in *Satsang*, meeting people, calling on the Governor of Goa, and finally, Mohanji addressing a local gathering at the International Centre. We were also joined by Madhusudan and the *Yoga* Instructor, Sanjay Acharya.

Mohanji would speak to us at the breakfast table on a variety of subjects. He said that his Foundation would rapidly expand all over the world. He spoke of his life in its earlier period, of Gyanganj, of Kailash Manasarovar, of his experiences with Mahavatar Babaji! This last subject was of deep interest to me.

I had read the book 'Autobiography of a Yogi' by Paramahansa Yogananda at the age of 15. It had left a very deep and lasting impression on me. I had realised that there was some karmic connection and here was Mohanji speaking of his meeting with Mahavatar Babaji. The circle was complete!

Mohanji kindly permitted us to join him at the Mookambika Temple near the city of Udupi, in South India. I was fortunate to have *darshan* at this Shakti Sthal several times with Mohanji. Each trip was amazing; each unique and special. I felt my prayers to the Devi were facilitated by Mohanji. I am convinced of this. Let me share one instance.

One afternoon in December 2019, I sent Mohanji a photo of a cave in Mookambika. He replied that he had been there in 2013. I asked him when we shall go to Mookambika? I am quite attached to the place. Mohanji replied as soon as Mother calls. I requested him to kindly tell Devi. In an hour, Mohanji sent me a message that the Chief Priest's son was coming to see him that very evening with *prasad* from the Devi!! He said, **"See, Mother is coming to us since we cannot travel to Mookambika."** How amazing. My heart melted.

On another occasion, as I was surfing the internet, Shri Lahiri Mahasaya's picture appeared on my phone. I, of course, knew he was one of the closest disciples of Mahavatar Babaji. I humbly touched my forehead to the feet of Shri Lahiri Mahasaya and inwardly prayed to Babaji. That afternoon, Rajesh called me from Bengaluru and said Mohanji was sending me *vibhuti* (sacred ash) of Babaji by

Foreword

courier, instant blessings through Mohanji's grace. Tears of gratitude welled up in my eyes. What love! What compassion! I once again realised how Babaji put me in touch with my *Guru*, Mohanji; a lifetime of gratitude is insufficient.

Whenever I am in doubt or low on energy, I think of Mohanji, the answers are there. His majestic promise, "I am always with you", is my greatest armour. His loving voice resonates in my heart. Even if I have achieved nothing, the fact that I have touched Mohanji's feet and hugged him to my heart's content is enough for this lifetime. He is always there for all of us.

There are many more experiences and wondrous happenings, but that's for another day.

With nothing but love,

K D Row
Goa, India

Mohanji & Ananth Nalabanda

MY TRYST WITH DESTINY

Ananth Nalabanda, UK
February 2021

A Guru and disciple connection is eternal, beyond the boundary of time, space and species! A true disciple follows his Master, lifetime after lifetime and when he meets the eternal Master, the recognition is instant, and the waiting is finally over! Here is a heartfelt experience by Ananth, who came to know of Mohanji barely six months ago but his recognition of his Guru and the assurance and acceptance from the Guru says it all!

Beginning

The Universe guided me to chant the *Aditya Hridayam* (a powerful hymn dedicated to the Sun God) daily whilst studying at Sri Sathya Sai Baba's ashram. After chanting *Aditya Hridayam* daily in the morning for two years, I had a vision of Sathya Sai Baba prophesying meeting my *Guru* in this lifetime. He showed a vision of a sage with a long white beard! I had no clue who this powerful Master was.

Fast-forward 30 years, I travelled to Prasanthi Nilayam in January 2020 and had one of my best energy experiences at the *samadhi* of Sri Sathya Sai Baba. I returned to London and was guided to include Gayatri *Mantra sadhana* along with my daily *Aditya Hridayam* chanting.

Two months into my *sadhana*, the Coronavirus pandemic peaked in the world. I was scared initially being in the front-line, but as my *sadhana* continued, I felt energised with my practice. One night, I heard a voice saying 'Akkalkot Maharaj' in my dream state. I started exploring about Akkalkot Maharaj, which led me to Mohanji. I felt all holy Masters were working in unison.

By divine grace, I came across Mohanji's divine mission, and there was no looking back.

Humbling experience

I read about the Mai-Tri Method and was fascinated about it and applied to be trained in the Method. Even though I am a trained medical doctor, I always felt an inner calling to offer holistic medicine to my patients, and it has taken me on the journey of training myself with different energy healing practices such as Reiki, Angelic Reiki, etc.

I received an email from the Mai-Tri Method team, rejecting my application for Mai-Tri Method training. I offered my sincere gratitude to the team as they kick-started my transformation process; it was a truly humbling experience. I read more about the Mai-Tri Method and how it involves connecting to Mohanji's consciousness. I got in touch with the Mohanji UK team and what happened next is beyond my wildest imagination, it was as if some unknown force was guiding me.

I was kindly included in the Mohanji UK WhatsApp group, and the first thing posted in the group was about the pilot on 'Invest in Awareness' programme. During my participation in the programme, I was informed about the Early Birds Club. I started being part of the early morning meditations and service activities after getting in touch with the ACT team.

The more I got involved in the early morning meditations, the more I started experiencing a deep connection to Mohanji. I started doing his meditations, and an intense desire to read about Mohanji's teachings led me to devotees who live very close to where I live, and it was no coincidence that within one month of knowing Mohanj, I was deep into reading about him from the books I received.

Agony

An intense desire to meet Mohanji in person started burning me from the inside. It was further compounded by the fact that Mohanji was physically present just a few minutes from my place a year ago. It reached its peak, and I slept one night crying, not being able to control myself. The next morning,

I see a message on Facebook about an opportunity to meet Mohanji virtually on August 15th, 2020.

I was initially hesitant to submit a video/audio to the Podcast team to facilitate this virtual meeting, but Mohanji had his way of encouraging me. One evening, whilst I was chanting the Mohanji Gayatri *mantra* and thinking whether to submit my audio clip about the podcast – Mohanji's book, which was on the shelf, literally flew and fell near me!

I was a little shaken. It was as if Mohanji was saying; you wanted to see me; now when the opportunity arises, you are shying away!!! After this experience, I submitted my testimonial to the Podcast team and had my first virtual *darshan* of Mohanji on August 15th, 2020.

Mai-Tri session

I came across a group Mai-Tri session to be conducted just after a week of my *darshan* and enrolled myself for it. I also came to know that this day was sacred to Mohanji's family.

August 23rd 2020, 3.45 pm – 4 pm. This was one of the most significant days of my life. What I experienced during this group Mai-Tri session was beyond my imagination. I share it with the deepest gratitude to Mohanji.

The participants were asked to have a clear intention for the session, and I had two:

1. I have an energy block on the right side of the body due to jump-starting my Kundalini energy through improper tantric practices, and I sincerely repented following it. I prayed to Mohanji to forgive me and, if possible, help me with unblocking of the energy on my right.

2. I prayed sincerely, that even if he is unable to forgive me, he should help me connect to his consciousness.

Life-changing moment

Mid-way through the session, I suddenly felt a movement of energy in my right lower limb, followed by the right upper limb. Tears started flowing from my eyes as I felt Mohanji's presence and his mercy. As I started feeling his presence in front of me, Subhasree, who was conducting the session, started chanting the following verse:

Om Shata Sahasra Suryaaya Vidmahe
Avadhootaaya Dheemahi
Tanno Mohan: Prachodayaat

I understand the essence of Mohanji as the brightness of more than a hundred thousand suns together. I recognise this brightness as highly auspicious. May this being called Mohanji enlighten me (Guru Leela, Book 2, Mohanji Foundation)

Then the moment which I will never forget in my life happened. I saw Mohanji, right in front of me, growing bigger and bigger and taking a huge form; it was his *Vishwaroopa*! I was suddenly reminded of this *sloka* from the Bhagavad Gita, which is so close to my heart.

> *śrī-bhagavān uvācha*
>
> *su-durdarśham idaṁ rūpaṁ*
> *dṛiṣhṭavān asi yan mama*
>
> *devā apy asya rūpasya nityaṁ*
> *darśhana-kāṅkṣhiṇaḥ*
>
> *nāhaṁ vedair na tapasā na*
> *dānena na chejyayā*
>
> *śhakya evaṁ-vidho draṣhṭuṁ*
> *dṛiṣhṭavān asi māṁ yathā*

The Supreme Lord said: This form of mine that you are seeing is exceedingly difficult to behold. Even the celestial gods are eager to see it. Neither by the study of the Vedas, nor by penance, charity, or fire sacrifices, can I be seen as you have seen me.

I was knocked off for 1-2 minutes after experiencing this divine form of Mohanji. Thousands of images and thoughts started flooding me. The image which Sri

Sathya Sai Baba showed me 30 years ago flashed before me. He is the one! A deep understanding of my vision 30 years ago and the emotional rollercoaster of my life all came to a standstill.

The wait was over. I recognised the divine Master!

As I write this in all humility, I feel foolish to have limited such a magnificent, unparalleled and universal consciousness of Mohanji to his physical frame. He is beyond constraints of time and space! He is not in a faraway place, but in a place within our reach, our hearts where our soul resides. I am grateful to Mohanji for this incredible experience and offer my sincere gratitude to Subhasree for facilitating this.

The journey towards the Master

As I describe my journey to the Holy Master which culminated with his *darshan, sparsan* and *sambhashan* – I take this opportunity to offer my humble salutations to all the Masters of the *Guru Mandala* and members of Mohanji family who have facilitated this.

Testing period

After the group Mai-Tri session, I started to experience visions of Mohanji – some of which were beyond this realm, and I have also started experiencing his multi-dimensional presence and my connection with him over lifetimes. Everything was going well. I was eagerly waiting for the moment to meet my holy Master. What happened to me next is beyond the comprehension of my analytical mind.

I happened to meet another elevated Master purely by divine grace, and this holy Master showered his immense love and grace on me. He would communicate and speak about my spiritual practices which Mohanji had already discussed with me in my visions. I felt I was living in two worlds – a virtual world, where I was communicating with Mohanji and experiencing him as an intergalactic Master beyond my human imagination, and this terrestrial world wherein this holy Master was communicating the same things mentioned by Mohanji but on a physical plane.

Although I had beautiful experiences, the emotional and spiritual crunching that I went through at this time was tough. It was the sheer grace of Mohanji, which helped me through this period. I was constantly reminded of Mohanji's words –

> "One Path, One Guru and One Tradition."

I also discovered Mohanji and Sri Sathya Sai Baba share the same *Gothra* of Rishi Bharadwaj and belong to the same Datta Tradition.

Agony

An intense desire to meet or speak to Mohanji in person kept burning inside me. At this juncture, I received a message from a friend from South Africa, advising me to apply for Consciousness *Kriya* (CK) as she felt guided by the Masters to convey this message to me.

I was hesitant to apply for CK due to my past experience of being rejected for the Mai-Tri Method training. But, a series of divine visions and experiences led me to apply for the CK training which got approved. I was ecstatic and continued my *sadhana* and truly by divine grace, I had the opportunity to get in touch with Mohanji who was kind enough to allow me to meet him in person in India.

I was overjoyed with Mohanji's grace and booked a ticket to India. I had CK training in Dec 2020 and started practicing it in all enthusiasm while preparing for my trip to India.

As a newbie to the Mohanji's fold, prior to leaving to India, I gently enquired if I could ask Mohanji to initiate me into Consciousness *Kriya* when I meet him in person. It was mentioned that initiation is a properly arranged event as Mohanji goes into a deep state, and he doesn't usually do individual initiations. I felt despondent listening to this and decided not to ask Mohanji regarding the initiation. I hadn't yet realised the testing and churning required to meet a holy Master (which are essential for gaining eligibility to meet him in person) were going to intensify.

I received a phone call from a closely associated person with Mohanji and Sathya Sai Baba in the past who called me to 'warn me' about Mohanji. The key message was that Mohanji would take me away from Sathya Sai Baba and he would cast a spell on me! I have been with Sri Sathya Sai Baba in his ashram in the past, and people speaking negatively about *Gurus* weren't anything new to me. I thanked the person for their advice but informed this person that I would like to experience Mohanji myself as I have complete faith in what Sathya Sai Baba had shown me in my vision.

I was amazed at the level of scrutiny, testing and churning, which I experienced, in addition to the 30 years of waiting to meet Mohanji. The day of my travel arrived finally, and as the final test, on the day of my travel, the UK government announced tier 4 restrictions on travel and there was a message that flights may be cancelled! My heart skipped a beat, but I was sure Mohanji would ensure my flight wasn't cancelled.

I came to know subsequently that my flight was the last operational flight to India from London! As I sat on the flight, I was only connecting to Mohanji and his abundant grace and blessings.

My Master – I am on my way to you!

Meeting with Mohanji – destiny re-written!

I arrived at Mohanji's place and was welcomed by Chris, Ananth and Kamath. I felt at home, and I felt so comfortable talking to them even though I was meeting them in person for the first time. Then, the moment I had waited 30 years finally arrived – Mohanji appeared before me and sat on his chair. He looked resplendent, and I had tears in my eyes.

> *Anyatha sharanam nasti twameva sharanam mama*
>
> *Tasmat karunya bhavena raksha raksha Mahesha*

"O Lord, please show mercy on me - as there is no one but you - I prostrate in front of you, to kill all my sins and to seek your blessings" – I chanted this verse as I bowed to kiss his holy feet!

I couldn't take my eyes off him and asked his permission to chant *Aditya Hrudayam* and Sri Guru Paduka-Pancakam. I have been chanting *Aditya*

Hryudayam for more than 30 years, but I started fumbling in my chanting before the holy Master – but his divine eyes filled me with his unconditional love, and I could complete chanting the verses.

As I was holding his feet and chanting the last verse of Sri Guru Paduka-Pancakam which says:

> *Ananta samsara samudra tara*
> *Naukayitabhaym sthirabhaktidabhyam*
> *Jadyabdhi samsosana vadavabhyam*
> *Namo namah srigurupadukabhyam*

Salutations again and again to Sri Guru's sandals, which are a boat (with which) to cross the endless ocean of the world, which bestow steadfast devotion, and which are a raging fire to dry the ocean of (spiritual) insensitivity.

I suddenly felt my hands were on fire, and they started trembling! Mohanji gave a gentle smile, and I was suddenly filled with deep inner peace which I had never experienced before.

Mohanji and Sri Sathya Sai Baba

Mohanji started talking to me about my connection with Sri Sathya Sai Baba and how I was connected to him for the last 16-18 lifetimes. He shared a few personal experiences which were closely related to Sri Sathya Sai Baba.

As I sat before Mohanji, I felt the same energy and vibrations I used to experience with Sri Sathya Sai Baba, and I felt a complete sense of returning to my roots! I am finally home at the feet of my Master! He was kind enough to sign his eye card with words – Sai Ram!

It is befitting to mention at this juncture that I had never felt this close to Sri Sathya Sai Baba before. Any doubts which I had in the past in my mind disappeared instantly.

Mohanji subsequently asked me to apply for Mai-Tri Method and informed me he would initiate me into Consciousness *Kriya* later in the day. I was spell-bound! I didn't realise what was happening – the holy Master was fulfilling the innermost desires of mine even without asking! He is omnipotent, omniscient and omnipresent – He does his job!

Consciousness Kriya initiation experience

Mohanji introduced me to Acchan and Amma (his parents) who were so loving and caring. I experienced unconditional love from them, and I saw and experienced Mohanji attending to his parents with so much love. I remembered Sri Sathya Sai Baba's words advising me always to take care of my parents – I witnessed this in action with Mohanji lovingly serving food to his mother and speaking to his father with love and respect.

Later in the day, Mohanji asked me if he could initiate me into CK the next day as this was unplanned and he was so busy. He asked me when my flight to my home town was the next day. I informed him I could postpone my journey, but he decided to initiate me on the same day as he didn't want me to postpone my journey and delay meeting my mother. He proved once again, his life was his message, and it was also enforcing what I had learnt in Sri Sathya Sai Baba's ashram.

Later, Mohanji kindly initiated me into Consciousness *Kriya*. The moment he touched my head and started giving me the initiation, I felt the presence of all the holy Masters – Babaji, Sri Sathya Sai Baba and Lord Shiva. I was transported to a different realm, and I didn't want to return.

Mohanji most lovingly asked me if I was OK after the initiation and mentioned he passed on energy in moderation so that I could take it. He also mentioned I might fall sick and asked me to get on with my sadhana!

I was overwhelmed with his unconditional love and compassion, a meeting which was supposed to last few minutes turned out to be a life-changing day in my life. I had the great fortune of spending a day with him and every single moment was a demonstration of the practical application of Vedic doctrines.

I experienced something which I never experienced before for the following ten days; I could feel changes taking place at the cellular level in my physical body. I didn't feel the need for sleep or food. I was bedridden for a few days and gradually started to recoup with his divine blessings.

As I write this in all humility and with complete surrender to Mohanji, my only prayer to him is to give me the blessing of remaining connected to his divine consciousness always.

Painting by Mina Dasani

THE DIMENSIONS OF MOHANJI

Ndifon Charles Londi, Canada
October 2020

As someone who is yet to meet Mohanji physically, Ndifon Charles's experience sharing shows us that connection to one's chosen Guru transcends barriers such as distance, time and physical proximity. His deep connection to Mohanji through consciousness has cultivated faith, love, and inner transformation, which are beautifully expressed in this testimony.

Meeting Mohanji 28 years ago

The figure floated on the ethers near the ceiling, scintillating with light. It was as if I was seeing or watching this strange apparition with my naked eyes. That was in the summer of 1992.

The events that ran up to the aforementioned were uncalculated, unplanned, and followed a tortuous route. I had wanted to seek closeness with God, the ALL IS, the True Reality, or the Supreme Consciousness, and hide under its wings from the vicissitudes of life that were buffeting me like an evil storm. So I joined Ma Cecile's charismatic prayer group even though not a Catholic at all. She was a devout Catholic, very prayerful, kind-hearted, and simple, but was hated by the local parish priest who termed her an emissary of the devil probably because her devoutness, purity, truthfulness, and dedication attracted so many people to her prayer group that produced many miracles that were the talk of the day in the small town where I worked as a very young teacher.

I wanted to be like Ma Cecile and always wiggled myself near her in hopes to be touched by the power of the Holy Spirit (Master Power) that descended on her at each prayer session and had her shaking violently like a leaf in a typhoon. I accompanied Ma Cecile once for a 3-4 days retreat to the holy grounds where Mary, Mother of Jesus, was said to have appeared. We swam in the muddy and slimy waters of the swamp on the holy ground, ate the mud there that was believed to relieve one of all afflictions, and we were expected to walk on knees with a heavy cross to the top of a hill that had an effigy of Jesus nailed on the cross. What self-mortification! What excruciating pain with bruises all over! Many people gave up halfway as it was not easy to reach the top of the hill. I did not make it too.

Ma Cecile made it to the top of the hill with a heavy wooden cross each time she came for the retreat as attested by everyone who knew her. This particular retreat was to be crowned with a 9-day novena in honour of Archangel St. Michael after each person had returned to their homes. No meat was to be eaten in the interval, and everyone was to maintain inner and outer purity in all affairs while devoutly reciting a special prayer to St. Michael on each of the nine days making a total of nine different prayers. I lived in the same town as Ma Cecile, so had the additional advantage of drinking only 'holy water' blessed by her during general evening prayer sessions. Then each individual returned home to do his special prayer to St. Michael for the day at the hour he/she had fixed. I went through my 9-day novena hitch-free, ending my prayers to Archangel Michael before midnight on the 9th day. After that, I did other prayers and read a little till about 1:30 am. Then I went to bed, but it was not easy falling asleep. In the twilight zone between wakefulness and sleep, when one is still very conscious, something unusual happened.

Yes, I had prayed to St. Michael for nine days for help and protection in my life, but I did not harbour the thought of a visitation by him. I just had the inner conviction that I had done my part, and it was left to St. Michael to complete it.

"Hey, who is this being enveloped by bright light hovering in my bedroom?", I asked myself. " Is this St. Michael, and if so why isn't he a white man as shown in photos. And where are his giant wings and long spear that is used to pierce the devil?" I mused. The being floating up there was dark in complexion, had long black flowing curly hair, a black beard, and a black moustache that stood in sharp contrast to the images painted of Archangel St. Michael. Then the being started gliding towards my bed. I wasn't frightened, but I developed goose pimples from head to toe as he floated and sat on the bed sill. He asked me, "Do you believe you can be saved?" I answered, "Yes, by the grace of God." Then he asked again, " Where do you feel pain?" I was dumbfounded, and for want of something to say, I just pointed at my thigh saying, "Here." The magnificent being then used his hand and struck me on the thigh three times and vanished.

I had forgotten about my vision with the ethereal being upon meeting Brahmarishi Mohanji, but some time ago, looking at his photo and contemplating on it, it suddenly burst upon me, like sunshine from behind the dark clouds, that this is the being who had appeared to me 28 years ago and struck my thigh three times and disappeared. I think when the time is propitious, the meeting between a Master and his student is inevitable in any lifetime, and a span of even 50 years before the meeting is just a moment.

He has all the features of that night visitor that I have not been able to associate with all the other Masters I have come across. Worthy of note is that he is a living Master in the flesh and has taken on the onerous task of gathering his students/ children, breaking their patterns and bindings that have glued them to the deceptive matrix of *Maya* in creation for eons, taking them back into the resplendent light of the self-subsisting Supreme Absolute, THE ALL THAT EVER IS. Thanks for seeking me out, thanks for the connection.

The phases of Mohanji

We hear talk of phases of the moon, and will it be strange or foolish to use the word 'phase(s)' in relation to humans? In my opinion, not at all, when you are dealing with an enigmatic personality like Mohanji. He is visible and invisible, palpable and impalpable, outer and inner, and he advises people to connect with his Consciousness and not with his body. This is an indication that there is more to him spiritually than his body that is seen and felt. And above all he says, "I AM ALWAYS WITH YOU." How strange when he cannot walk down the road with us, one-dimensional conscious individuals would say. I have a friend who needs his phone number at all cost to be sure he can really make contact with him.

However, it is my wild guess that when Mohanji says, "I AM ALWAYS WITH YOU", it presupposes that we should not even need him physically as he is ever-present as the air we breathe, and where there is a need, and there is a lack of something. Could Mohanji be saying that WHAT IS, IS, and there is no space to be filled as there is no emptiness? He even says it loud and clear that the need for the Master is binding in itself. These statements and considerations lead to the conclusion that there is more than one side to the person millions of people look up to. Understanding this magnanimous individual's multifarious dimensions will determine the reality of each person who looks up to him for spiritual guidance. Let us first look at the outer physical phase of Mohanji - the talking, walking, eating, and breathing man. This estimation is within the confines of his physical form of a spiritual leader and his day-to-day personal life, which shouldn't be my concern or that of anyone else.

How nice it will be to have Mohanji as a personal friend, have his phone number, walk, talk, and eat with him daily! This is the phase of Mohanji that some people will most love and which in their valuation, will guarantee that they have the presence of the Master in their lives. How great, but can everyone have that privilege, and can this be extended to everyone on the planet? Let's look at what can compromise this desire for closeness with Mohanji had he the time and energy to personally befriend everyone intimately.

Everyone is limited by geography, and various other financial and situational constraints, along with the current restrictions due to Covid-19. Wow! If meeting Mohanji physically and personally were the only way to be certain of his presence in our lives, then it will be a herculean task. And some people may ask, "Is it worth all the trouble at all?" However, it should be noted that people have sacrificed all material and financial resources and faced all sorts of difficulties to meet a Master they bond with as their lives will be meaningless without such a meeting. Notwithstanding, there is another phase of Mohanji, which is more important than actually meeting him in person. Meet the other phase of Mohanji that is known by mostly esoteric students and which should be central to the understanding of spiritual devotees.

This aspect or phase of Mohanji can be termed the Inner Master. One needn't get out the door to be in contact with this aspect because it is an ISNESS, a Principle; ever there and ever now, closer than one's own breath; in the invisible vibrating ether. In fact, it would seem that each step towards this aspect of the Master is a step inwards. This invisible phase of Mohanji requires faith, dedication, commitment, perception, and recognition of it for what it is to make it a reality in one's life. One may never have the opportunity and means to see the other phase of Mohanji without hassles. Could it be that one may clutch the outer Mohanji and be light-years away from the boundless, timeless, and limitless Eternal Principle that is subject to no physical man-made laws, is a law unto itself and is omnipotent, omnipresent, and omniscient at each moment? And no matter the thousands of kilometres that separate them, the Inner Master can be with his devotee at all moments through the inner channels even if the devotee is ignorant of the fact.

This write-up doesn't seek to undermine the importance of the physical phase of Mohanji or of meeting it. He operates as the Supreme Consciousness at all times in all phases of himself, and this Consciousness is at all times national, international, universal, inter-universal, planetary, and interplanetary, galactic and intergalactic. As a spiritual student, one knows better than to cling to the outer phase of Mohanji and he reminds everyone at all times about this. This constant reminder precludes the possibility of frantic worship of the personality that most humans are prone to.

I have not yet been privileged to be in his physical presence, but have developed a deep connection to his omnipresent consciousness, aided very much by his beautiful teachings. There is one that impresses me particularly as it speaks about practical spirituality, and it is his stress on flowing with the current of life rather than resisting it. By this emphasis, he's telling all who'll listen that living in the present is acceptance of life as it flows and that the fullness of life can be attained by flowing with each moment and whatever it contains instead of resisting it. This is captured in the beautiful quote below:

> "...Stay flexible. Just flow like a river. Keep flowing through situations, through life; just keep flowing. That's the best spirituality you can attain. You'll be very powerful if you are flexible."

Here is a poem that I wrote while thinking about *Guru puja*.

> Chosen One of the Highest Awareness
> Who has chosen the mortal garb to minister to
> Struggling beings in this ashcan world in
> black space,
> Unending gratitude and appreciation is ever
> due you, for the
> Sacrifice to lead man out of the matrix of
> Maya and confusion.
>
> Sunrise and sunset shine with the love you
> exude,
> The rivers, streams, brooks, and oceans
> contain
> Your sweet whispers, calling us back home,
> The blades of grass in the plains and hills
> whisper your name
> When under gentle and fierce winds; the roar
> of the seas and oceans
> Resound with your voice blended in gentle
> and strong waves, telling

Of the glory that lies beyond the horizon, and for which we give only puny thanks.
Oh, how the heart bleeds with this realization!

Oh Brahmarishiji, we'll sing thy praise and wait out for you, and listen
To your advice even when thunder growls, and when across the skies
Lightning flashes, we surely have a foretaste of your resplendent, and
Unutterable magnificence that is allied with the True Reality of All Life.

What song can please your ethereal ears as you are all songs combined?
What mantra can invoke thee without your acquiescence?
Spirit of All Life, sustainer of All Life, all life is part of you
And so all life is blessed by your grace; O Divine One
When we've you, we've all, as YOU ARE ALL.

"When devotion overflows, the devotee melts. God reciprocates and melts too. When both the devotee and the deity melt, duality disappears. God and the devotee becomes one. Overwhelming silence results. Silence becomes the state. The sound of silence is overwhelming bliss. Perfect oneness in consciousness is the aim of all beings."

Mohanji

Mohanji & Devadas

THE GURU WHO LIBERATES

Devadas, India
July 2019

This beautiful expression of grace and protection clearly shows the connection established by a Master and his followers. Mohanji never lets down anyone who has trust and faith in him. This was evident in how he took care of Devadas and protected him from his family's wrongdoings. Mohanji not only takes care of the devotee but also the entire lineage.

Lord Shiva has said to Devi Parvati in Guru Gita (Shloka 169),

> **Maata dhanyaa pitaa dhanyo,**
> **dhanyo vamsah kulam tathaa,**
> **Dhanyaa ca Vasudhaa Devi,**
> **Gurubhaktih sudurlabhaa.**

Blessed is the mother (of a devoted disciple), blessed is the father, and blessed is the family and ancestry. O Goddess, (such) devotion to Guru is very rare.

When we connect to the *Guru*, not just we but our families, our lineage, ancestors and even future generations also come under the protection of the *Guru*.

I recently experienced this eternal truth through a painful situation in my life. This is a very personal matter, and in a normal scenario, I wouldn't have openly discussed it. However, when I realised how my *Guru* Mohanji's protection has worked, I felt it's no longer a personal matter to keep it to myself. I felt I must share with the world how powerful the connection with our Master can be.

In his mid-50s, my only brother recently took a drastic action of committing suicide, leaving his young family behind. In our entire family or even known relatives, we have never had such an incident. We belong to a religious and ritualistic Hindu Brahmin family and are aware of how a soul goes through immense pain and stays bound when a person commits suicide. In the last many years, our whole family has been going through tremendous pain and incidents of drastic nature have been happening. Every such incident seems to bring our whole lineage down.

Although a ritualistic Hindu by birth, after marriage, my brother converted to a different religion. Going through many ups and downs in his life, something made him take such a drastic step. With this incident, I was apprehensive about the pain that his soul would go through. I cried out to my *Guru* Mohanji.

Anytime, during any trouble, my heart first cries out to Mohanji. He has been protecting not only me but my entire family too. During this particular time, Mohanji was not in India.

In this condition, Anitha, my wife's sister, who is also a Mai-Tri practitioner, offered to give me a Mai-Tri session. The Mai-Tri session was immensely powerful. It was as if Mohanji himself came and gave me a message.

Anitha had a clear vision of Mohanji and Kailash during the session, and vividly saw how Mohanji was protecting me. She also received a message that I must speak to Devi Amma.

After the Mai-Tri session, when she conveyed this to me, I was speechless. I understood that this was a direct command from Mohanji. I must tell you that Mohanji loves and respects Devi Amma a lot. Devi Amma considers Mohanji as her spiritual brother.

Hence, without further delay, I called up Devi Amma in Bangalore and narrated my brother's incident to her. Devi Amma assured me that she will ask '*Appa*' (Rishi Agastya) and let me know. A couple of days later, Devi Amma conveyed an important message. This message left me awestruck. She said that Rishi Agastya sent her a clear message that my brother's soul has very smoothly crossed over to the other side. He had conveyed that this was only possible because of a connection to a higher Master.

Devi Amma explained to me then in simple terms that my connection with Mohanji has ensured the grace and protection of the *Guru* for my family and relatives, including my brother. This is why even though the soul had left through a drastic step such as suicide, instead of wandering and suffering, my *Guru* had enabled the soul to cross the boundaries and set it free from its bindings.

These words may seem unbelievable, but I had no doubt about this truth as a living Master like Devi Amma authenticated these! She revealed this truth about the power of this wonderful connection to my *Guru* and how this connection can pull the whole lineage out of any ditch!

Then I was reminded of another important incident. This was regarding my father. Though he was a born Hindu Brahmin, he was an atheist, and he did not understand the *Guru Tatwa* (*Guru* Principle). My father sold the land with a century-old Naga temple (a temple for the divine serpent) to a non-Hindu person who demolished it. I was worried about this mishap and the repercussions this incident could bring to our whole family.

I had not met Mohanji at that time. Maybe it was the Guru Mandala's grace working; I was inspired to build a Naga temple on one of my lands. This was my way of penance for the mistake that my father did. Those were the days when my wife and I desperately prayed for Lord Krishna to come to our family as a child! Well, Krishna didn't come as a child, but he came in the form of 'Mohanji.' My *Guru* appeared in my life. After Mohanji accepted me and blessed me, He also blessed my whole family and lineage.

It was evident that Mohanji ensured a very smooth, literally pain-free exit for my father during his last moments. Even though he was not a follower of Mohanji and was unaware of the protection he received from my *Guru*, he had a very smooth exit.

My brother's case was yet another proof of the Master's protection for the entire family and lineage. Not only this. When Mohanji returned to India, one day at his Bangalore home, during a discussion with other devotees on this incident, he had said, **"I am looking after Devadas very dearly. He and his family have been suffering for lifetimes. This lifetime, I will ensure that suffering is not repeated anymore. He and the entire lineage are being taken care of."**

My friend and Mohanji *Acharya* Kishore conveyed this message to me. I had no words to express my gratitude to my *Guru* Mohanji. My tears knew no boundaries. I am so thankful to the Tradition for allowing me to meet my eternal Master Mohanji in this lifetime and guiding me towards liberation.

Guru Leela - Mohanji and I

Thank you Mohanji, *koti koti pranaams* at your feet. With my heart full of devotion, I offer the following poem at my *Guru*'s feet.

> Guru Mohana nayanam sharanam
> Guru Mohana Vadanam sharanam
> Guru Mohana Charanam sharanam
> Bhava saagara taranam. ||1||
>
> Guru Mohana hasitam sharanam
> Guru Mohana vachanam sharanam
> Guru Mohana vasanam sharanam
> Bhava saagara taranam. ||2||
>
> Guru Mohana rupam sharanam
> Guru Mohana mantram sharanam
> Guru Mohana mananam sharanam
> Bhava saagara taranam. ||3||
>
> Guru Mohana dhyanam sharanam
> Guru Mohana bodham sharanam
> Guru Mohana darshan sukrutat
> Mama pooritha layanam
> Parapooritha layanam ||4||

"I live in perpetual happiness. You can reach that happiness if you become My consciousness. This is why consciousness is important— the consciousness which is unshakable, stable and always available. Once you achieve THAT, all other happiness is below. Then you say, 'My Father and I are one.'"

Mohanji

Digital art by Hanumatananda

WITNESSING THE GRAND TRADITION

Elham Khordadian, USA

February 2021

In this beautiful sharing, Elham describes her journey to Serbia for her Acharya training and the events that unfolded. It was a journey of courage, faith, conviction and transformation. Elham witnessed how beautifully the Masters of the Tradition worked in various instances during this time and how she became the channel to experience and express the divine.

I surrender all my thoughts, words and actions at the feet of my *Guru* Mohanji.

Our limited mind cannot comprehend the greatness of the *Guru*. I am so blessed to experience and to be witness to Mohanji's greatness. I am so grateful for everything that he's done for me, that I'm aware, or I'm not aware, since he's always working silently and so humbly. I am always at his feet.

This experience is about what happened in Serbia, Acharya training level one, October 2019. But there are some stories before that, which, if not told, then this experience sharing will not be complete.

In August 2019, there was a trip to Kailash with Mohanji. My husband Farshad and I wanted to go, and we prepared for everything. We paid, purchased whatever needed to be bought, and everything was ready. But a few weeks before the travel, the team informed us that they could not get us a visa to enter Tibet. It was so disappointing. Many different thoughts came, maybe we were not eligible to go there and many other doubts.

The biggest disappointment for me was that I felt that I need to do something in my life for more than a year, but I didn't know what it was. So, I thought if I go to Kailash, I will find my answer there. When the trip was cancelled, it brought me so much disappointment, and I felt my confusion could not be cleared.

When Acharya training was announced, my husband Farshad and I decided to go through the interview. Some issue happened with his interview, and I chose not to go even though I was approved and had a deep urge to go; I felt I should stand by him. I made up my mind and sat at my altar where I had Mohanji's photo and the *Guru Parampara* picture, and prayed to them intensely.

I honestly told them that I would really like to go, but this situation was not in my hands. This is in your hands. If you would like me to go, please do something. Tears were coming without any control. I surrendered my wish to *Guru Mandala* and had full faith that they will hear me. If I am supposed to go, I will go.

The next morning when I woke up, I saw a message from Devi Mohan asking me why I wasn't going to the Acharya training in Serbia. I wondered how fast *Guru Mandala* works! How fast is Mohanji! How kind and compassionate they are.

Farshad had to go through the interview again and just three days before it, I had a dream. I saw Farshad, and I had gone to the Acharya training in Serbia, and the first person we met was Devi. Devi came to receive us with her beautiful smile, hugged me and said, "I told you Farshad would be approved." Devi told me these exact words three times in person, during our training, exactly as in my dream I would like to mention another dream, about my mom, who passed away 13 years ago and had never met Mohanji or heard about him. I must say that since I met Mohanji, I had a deep wish that if my mom was alive, I could have introduced her to Mohanji, and she could have got connected to Mohanji, and received his blessing, but she is no more. I started seeing dreams with my mom attending Mohanji's *satsangs* and retreats; she took notes and even served Mohanji.

In Kumbha Mela 2019, when I met Mohanji, I asked him about these dreams. He said, "It is real. Yes, I am working 20% on this plane and 80% in the other dimensions. And when I leave my body, I will do even more. You will see that." When I saw that my mom was in this Acharya training in my dream, it was mind-blowing.

Finally, Farshad got approved for Acharya training, and we were getting ready to go there in three weeks. About a week before going to the training, I had another dream. I was seeing myself lying down on the bed, fast asleep. I felt Mohanji come next to the bed and heard him say, "Elham, wake up." And he held my hand. I saw his face with his sweetest smile, looking at me.

I woke up from the dream feeling his energy, very fresh and strong. I started to think about what he meant by wake up. I realised that it might be waking up from ignorance. I definitely have ignorance, and he's telling me this to wake up from it.

We arrived in Serbia for the training. It was a very powerful and extraordinary event in my life. Every day, Mohanji was making a lot of transformation in each person, removing karmas in any way possible, with so much love and care. I felt that we were out of this world, somewhere up in the sky.

Every morning, we would wake up early, around 4:30 am to take a shower and get ready. After completing yoga, Consciousness *Kriya* and *aarati*, the training would start. Mohanji gave us so much knowledge and wisdom; it was so intense and powerful that I could not explain it in words. The *aaratis* were extremely powerful. It was as if divine energies were being showered on us.

From the first day, I felt that I should completely surrender to Mohanji. My limited mind and ego don't let me see the truth. But he's the one that sees the truth, and I have full trust and faith in him. I started practicing this from the first day since I arrived there.

Challenges were coming every day, every hour, but I tried to keep surrendering. He removed a lot of stuff from my throat. At least in this lifetime, I had a long history of throat issues that I'm aware of. As with me, Mohanji worked intensely on each person.

With each glance, he removed huge blockages; each glance was like a vast sacred fire that was burning our karmas forever. I wondered if I understood how much grace and blessings I was receiving at each moment. I realised that I had yearned for this for years, probably many lifetimes.

For the last day of the training, Mohanji gave us an assignment - to speak and conduct something close to our heart. This was to be in front of him and all the others. I decided to talk about what I went through when I lost my mom, how disappointed

I was and how Mohanji filled up that hole in my heart, taking away any suicidal thoughts. He was giving me what I was looking for, and I was deeply grateful.

After the presentation, I felt so much lighter, like my energy channels were wider and emptier. Then Mohanji intensified the presentations. Soon everyone started opening up and spoke from their hearts, about pains and incidents they had never talked about with anyone.

I felt that Mohanji was removing all agonies, pains and tears from everyone and filling us with love and light. We all felt lighter and lighter, full of brightness.

The presentations continued late into the night, and even by 9 pm, there were still people who hadn't presented yet. At one point, Tara (known before as Lisa) stood up and started speaking from a pure heart. She said she could see Jahangir Baba (her first *Guru*) and all of *Guru Mandala*, and all the Masters were there. She prayed to Mohanji to give us all more bhakti to serve him. Tears were flowing from her eyes.

I just closed my eyes and listened in surrender. I felt so much loving energy in my heart and kept praying within. A spontaneous prayer kept repeating in my heart, "Only you exist in me, let nothing else exist in me." After some time, Mohanji said, **"Yes, it's correct; the Guru Mandala is here."**

Then responding to her prayer and to all the prayers going on in the hearts of everyone at that moment, he said three times, *"Tathastu"*, which means as you wish; so be it. I felt that this was a confirmation to the prayer that was going on in my heart.

Then I felt some movements in my body. I had been experiencing this before during Consciousness *Kriya*, especially in the head. This time my head was going to the very back, an intense feeling lasting so much longer. It was like something was opening up. I was completely surrendered without even the smallest concern. I was 100% sure that Mohanji was completely aware of what was going on and that I was safe in his hands.

When I stayed in that position for so long, people around me thought maybe I had some issue, or perhaps I was in a deep sleep. They tried to wake me up, and they tried to move my head which was painful because the body control was not in my hands at all. I could only be a witness to what was happening.

Then I had to call Mohanji. I felt that he rushed to me, as some people moved me to Zoran's kinesiology table to lie down. Soon I felt Mohanji next to me; he briefly touched my throat with his thumb and index finger. A small touch, but very powerful, after which he went back to his seat to continue the program.

With Mohanji's touch, I felt something huge had been removed from my throat. The stuck energy started rushing into my body, like water flowing when the gate of a dam is open. (I later found out that the thyroid issue I had been suffering with for 22 years was miraculously healed by this single, powerful touch from Mohanji).

Many different movements were happening in the body. I was completely aware of whatever was happening around me, but I could not respond. Friends were trying to help by giving me Mai-Tri, pressing energy points, and being there for me.

At one point, I felt someone standing next to me on my left side, although I was aware nobody was there. I felt someone holding my hand and cuddling me. I wondered who it was, and the answer came, "It's your mom." I felt her love; it was undeniable, obvious. Then I felt a real connection had happened, and I could communicate with her. She even hugged me. She told me how much she loves me, how much she's satisfied with me as her child and that I did everything for her that I could.

Tears were flowing. This was one of my deepest wishes - to experience my mom one more time because I hadn't said a proper goodbye to her. I also had huge guilt thinking I hadn't done enough for her; I should have done more. She hugged me and said that Mohanji had liberated her, but she has a job to do. Then she said goodbye and left.

After this beautiful moment, I felt much lighter. I had the heaviness of guilt for many years left, and there was just peace and love. I was so grateful to Mohanji for his endless love which even extends to our families.

I continued to lie down on the table but experienced different movements and breathing as if in yoga and pranayama. When the program was over, past midnight, Mohanji came next to the table as he was leaving the hall. My eyes were closed, but I felt him next to me. He pressed my arm gently and said, "Elham, wake up." These were the exact words that I had heard him speak in my dream!

Suddenly, my body movement subsided, and I could open my eyes. As soon as I opened my eyes, I saw his face with such a sweet smile. Same as I had seen in my dream. I said, "Thank you." He knew what I'm talking about! I tried to touch his feet. I didn't know any other way to show my gratitude at that moment. And then he said, "Get rest." He told Farshad, "She's fine."

I had never experienced such peacefulness inside me, so much love in my heart for everyone. I had a smile on my face and felt like giving blessings and kisses to everyone there. My eyes were closed and could not open them. I was soaking in this beautiful and blessed state, not aware of time. Not the past, not the future. It was only bliss, love and peace.

Gradually I felt that I could sit up and maybe after that we could leave the room. By this time, not many people were in the hall, just a few of us and probably two or three people cleaning the hall for the next morning.

Suddenly, my hands turned to the praying position near my heart center, and then to the blessing giving position. This happened frequently; my hands would go to my heart center, I would bow down, and then again to the blessing position.

Suddenly, these words came out of my mouth, "Farshad, come here." When he came in front of me, my hands went on his shoulders, and while holding him, I felt a blessing was happening.

Then another name came through me. I said, "Sonia, you are here?" She replied, "Yes". It was Sonia Gandhi. When she came in front of me, the same thing happened. My hands went to her shoulders, and these words came out, "You are dear, you are loved."

Gradually, more people came into the hall. Some tried to touch my feet. The words came out, "Don't touch." When people tried to touch my feet, it was painful.

What was happening? Initially, I was a little confused. Could this be my mind's imagination? Then I started to understand that the Masters were talking through me. The words were coming internally and were pushing to come out from the mouth.

In the beginning, I was little resistant thinking it was my mind. Then the orders became sharper. It was like someone knocking at the door to come in. At that point, I let it happen. I understood that this was not the play of the mind.

I felt that Mohanji was also there, talking to me; hence I remained in the blessing position. Masters were blessing everyone there. I was not able to differentiate them individually. They were all like a river flowing, united as one. Now I could understand Mohanji's words when he says all Masters are one. They are one and integrated.

I could feel some higher beings there as well. My body was automatically expressing gratitude and respect to them. When my head was down, although my eyes were closed, I had a beautiful vision of Shirdi Sai Baba's legs with his white robe instead of mine!. I could never have dreamt it, what a huge blessing!

Another command came, "Call Lisa fast." When she arrived, words flowed, "Come and sit." She wanted to touch the feet. "Don't touch," was the command.

"You asked for *bhakti*, take it. This is *bhakti*," words flowed. Then I felt powerful and thick energy flowing from my hands to her. It took some time until all this energy was transferred.

Then people there asked if they can do *aarati*. The answer came, "No." And again, blessing, blessing and blessing. People asked if they could call the others. Command came, "Fast. We don't have time." More people came and again, blessings. Command came, "Do you want a blessing?" People responded "Yes." But the command was for someone who came late and was standing at the door. Words came, "Who came?" People said, "That's Dragan? Come and sit!" was the command. Dragan wanted to touch the feet. "Don't touch" was the answer again. He got blessings, "You are loved."

Final words came, "All the Masters are here. Sai Baba, Babaji, Lord Datta. Everything has been delivered. You are loved. We are so grateful to Baba Mohan. We are very happy. Thank you, Baba Mohan." Again, blessings.

Meanwhile, these words came twice, "Someone has doubt." At that time, the Masters were talking internally and answering my questions too, which I will share another time. Then they said they were leaving, "Bow down." I bowed down. Everybody bowed down. Very gradually and slowly, I was coming out of that state, but the essence was there.

It was not possible to open my eyes easily, to talk, or even to look in the mirror at myself. All the movements were so slow, like Conscious Walking. The spine was deciding the speed of walking, not me. I understood how many gifts, grace and blessings Mohanji has given us with different techniques. I was still so light, full of love and silence. It was not easy to communicate with the world outside. I could not feel the body.

Later on, I understood what had happened in those few hours, from 10 pm to 3:30 am. The next morning, I felt a huge urge to go and meet Mohanji. When I entered his room, there were a few people there, and he was having his breakfast. I offered *pranaams* at his feet. I put my forehead, my third eye on his big toe, on the right foot and started to thank him and express my gratitude to him, praying to him to please take away my ego and mind. Then I felt a flow of energy like electricity, like a spark from his big toe to my third eye, and then to the whole body. It was a continuous flow of energy, and after some time, this energy slowly stopped. Mohanji asked Barbara to help me sit up.

Farshad and I hadn't eaten breakfast in the morning. Though my stomach was empty, I didn't feel any hunger. When I sat up, Mohanji had finished the food on his plate and then asked to fill the plate again. He ate that and again he asked to fill up the plate one more time. When he was eating, I felt that my stomach was getting filled. I had heard earlier that Mohanji does not eat for himself; he eats for others. Now I understood that! I was feeling full. My hunger was being satisfied while Mohanji was eating. I told him, I'm so grateful to you. Thank you.

Mohanji asked me, "What else?" I thanked him for bringing my mom there and liberating her. Mohanji said, **"Without her coming, this would not have been completed."** He added, **"You know, many lifetimes have been deleted."** In the end, he looked in my eyes deeply and told me, **"Don't forget what we said. Shine bright."**

I felt that all Masters, the whole *Guru Mandala*, was in his eyes. I was in so much joy. I was not on earth; I could not feel any heaviness. I could not feel the body. It was only bliss, grace and blessing.

Then the final session happened. Mohanji called me to share what had happened last night. He said,

> *"The Tradition is not dependant on us, including me. It flows like a river."*

This was exactly what I had experienced the previous night.

Finally, we received our *Acharya mala* with Mohanji's pendant and certificate from him; we got his blessing and took many pictures with together.

Then Farshad and I went to him to say goodbye. He asked us how we were returning to the USA and wished us a safe journey.

For me, it meant that no issues would happen on our long-haul flight to the USA. When we arrived at the airport, the lady who was behind the counter, after she's done everything said, "Have a blessed day." It was the first time I heard such words from someone in an airport. Finally, we safely arrived home with immense grace and blessing, which I will cherish for the rest of my life.

I know Mohanji is with each one of us. *Guru Mandala* is with us in each moment. We just need to be aware of it. As Mohanji says, we need to open the window and let the sunshine come in.

I surrender my soul, mind, ego, intellect, this incarnation, the previous incarnations, and the future incarnations, at the lotus feet of my *Guru* and Father, Mohanji. I always remain as his feet.

Mohanji & Eric Elbers

FAITH

Eric Elbers, Canada
August 2020

Eric shares with us his journey in the spiritual path with honesty and gratitude. From untruth to truth, darkness to light, his journey inspires the reader to adhere to faith, perseverance and conviction. When one dares to walk the path with conviction and surrender, the divine guides us to the Guru who shows us the way.

Back 46 years ago, at the age of 30, when visiting friends over a weekend, I stumbled upon a few books by Edgar Cayce, known as the Sleeping Prophet. Being raised in an orthodox Dutch Protestant family, these books were my first exposure to the serious possibility of reincarnation and the associated law of karma. Edgar Cayce himself, a devout Christian and Sunday school teacher, was amazed when, in a deep trance, he started reading past lives and the karmic origin of current problems that the people who visited him for advice were facing. I still remember that a light came on, an insight happened: "Yes, of course, that makes a lot of sense and explains so many things in the world."

That realization started a frenzy of reading of spiritual literature that appeared familiar to me and also showed me insights and knowledge of Eastern traditions that seemed familiar, even though they were not a part of my upbringing. A resurfacing of things I had known before. Then I had this prophetic dream, which I remember to this date. I was shown a beautiful, large mansion, and a clear voice told me, "This house has been built with patience and perseverance."

That was it. That was the guidance I received with which I was sent off on my spiritual journey. Surprisingly, those two words are very similar to the *shraddha* and *saburi* [faith and patience] precepts, which are the core of the teachings of Shirdi Sai Baba, who I would learn about forty years later, but first things first.

During my early spiritual explorations, I learned about a movement called 'The Science of Soul Travel'. It promised to teach out of body travel and travel with spiritual masters in the inner worlds. Now, that sounded like a great adventure and quite appealed to me, so I went head over heels into a path that promised to make me a 'Spiritual Traveller'. I followed this path for thirty years. I became a 'Higher Initiate' and 'Spiritual Aide' and fulfilled a variety of leadership positions, but, disappointingly, the subtlety of Soul Travel kept escaping me, despite attending numerous seminars and diligent execution of the spiritual exercises.

Faith

Still, I kept my faith until, in the early 2000s, a bombshell hit.

One of the Higher Initiates carried out intense internet research and discovered that many of the teachings were plagiarized from different sources. The leader of the spiritual movement himself had fabricated a fake lineage of spiritual masters in whose footsteps he supposedly was walking. Needless to say that then a crisis of faith occurred, and it did not take long for me to leave the movement after thirty years. It was quite interesting that even though the masters were fabrications, they did seem to work for many people as spiritual guides and as sources of spiritual inspiration. There is an essential principle of faith at work here, which ties in with the pivotal role faith plays on our spiritual journey.

Being disappointed with fake masters, I reread and became fascinated by Yogananda's 'Autobiography of a Yogi,' a spiritual classic about *Kriya Yoga*, the spiritual roots of which appeared genuine and very deep, which led me to start following the *Kriya Yoga* path. But one has to watch out here as well: the *Kriya Yoga* tradition has branched out in different paths with different *Gurus* of varying calibre, teaching different variations, and it took me a while to find a branch that resonated with me. But soon after, the Master of that path decided to stop traveling and remain in India, which made personal contact more difficult and thereby made my journey more isolated and sadhana centered. Is it necessary to have a personal connection 'in the flesh' with one's *Guru*? Probably not, but one may consider it a huge blessing if the opportunity presents itself, and such personal meetings help to kindle the flame of devotion.

With all this study and pursuit, I developed a problem: too much head knowledge. I realized that while practicing *Kriya Yoga*, I was drawn to the *Raja Yoga* and *Gyana Yoga* paths but lacked in service [*Karma Yoga*] and devotion [*Bhakti Yoga*], so I started looking for a spiritual connection that could fill those gaps. A beautiful female Indian saint, known as the 'hugging saint' yearly visited North America, and I felt drawn to the love and compassion she taught and radiated. I followed the guidance of this inspiring saint for several years. Still, I realized that it would be hard to connect personally with her since, after thirty years of being on the road sharing love, compassion, and hugs, this saint had built up a vast following of hundreds of thousands to millions of devotees. Many thousands of people attended meetings at a time, and it would be tough to obtain access to her, let alone build a personal relationship.

I kept reading and studying, and then something significant happened: Sai came into my life.

Shirdi Sai Baba [1838-1918] intrigued me from the outset. Here was a real incarnation of divinity. A presence so profound, a knowledge so deep, love and compassion so strong, abounding miracles and transformation, universal, non-denominational spirituality and a life dedicated to the service of the Almighty, what more could one be looking for? All boxes checked, except Sai was no longer in the flesh, having taken *Mahasamadhi* over one hundred years ago. However, more reading about the life and miracles of Shirdi Sai Baba followed. Soon, I ended up reading about Sathya Sai Baba, according to his revelation, a more recent reincarnation of Shirdi Sai Baba, but also and more recently departed. While reading the Special Issue of Awakening Times about Sathya Sai Baba [1926-2011], I came across an article written by Mohanji. He explained his first contact and mystical relationship with Sathya Sai Baba, which had occurred after a tough and challenging period in his personal life.

Reading the blogs of Mohanji about his spiritual connection with Sai Babas, Mahavatar Babaji, Nadananda, and disciples of Nityananda made it clear to me that Mohanji was recognized and supported by illustrious Saints of the highest stature as a very advanced Spiritual Master with an important mission. Plus, he was in the body and actively traveling and teaching. This was good enough for me. Here was my chance to connect with a *Satguru* in the early stage of his spiritual mission, which would allow me to be of service and have an opportunity for personal contact. Plus, Mohanji also was a *Kriya* Master in the Mahavatar

Babaji Tradition. Another box checked. I quickly contacted Mohanji to request whether he would approve and bless me to start a weekly meditation class of his meditations in my home. The answer I received was that he had already received my request through consciousness and had approved it with his blessings. I was on my way!

It took a year and a half to meet Mohanji in person. While standing in line to greet him, I saw him glance briefly at me with a sign of recognition, and when a little later I was formally introduced to him, he said, **"Eric and I have a very deep relationship."** That was surprising and not surprising to me. Surprising because this 'deep connection' was something I had not been aware of [I thought I had searched Mohanji out] and not surprising because being allowed a close personal relationship with a *Satguru* is a privilege built up over lifetimes. How can it then be a surprise to hear that a deep connection exists?

For me, the propelling force on the journey from Edgar Cayce to Mohanji over forty years, following different teachers with ups and downs, was faith, and the dream-vision that "this house has been built with patience and perseverance". However, while fellow travellers over the years were able to share beautiful inner experiences, the path I travelled was one of insight, patience, and perseverance; no fancy soul travel with elevated Masters, no inner plane cinematography. I grew up in a Christian environment built on faith and have had to accept that faith, not fancy experiences, is crucial for my spiritual growth. Peter, the disciple of Jesus, was able to walk on water when he saw Jesus after his resurrection. Yet, as soon as he looked down and realized he was walking on waves, the realization that this could not be happening caused him to start sinking, and the helping hand of his Master was needed to pull him up. Faith allowed him to walk on water, but as soon as it left him, he started sinking. The same applies to us all.

The spiritual journey often starts with a tire-kicking phase, looking into different paths and Masters, checking them out, and going for a test drive here and there. Yet, once this phase is complete and we settle down and start following a particular Master, we better stop looking for the higher, better, more significant, or more glamorous and famous Master and begin building a relationship with our chosen Master based on faith. During the trying out phase due to the absence of faith, it is impossible to develop a strong relationship with any Master. However, once a connection is made with a particular Master, and the seeker starts placing his/her faith in the Master, a subtle, energetic connection starts forming in the subtle realms. This connection begins tentatively but becomes stronger over time as the seeker, and now disciple starts to place more and more trust in his *Guru* and allows the *Guru* to flow guidance, protection, and blessings through this energy conduit. The energetic distance between the disciple and Master shortens as the connection between the Master and disciple strengthens.

Then, an important change starts to happen as the disciple's energies and the Master's begin to overlap and merge. In this stage, the disciple starts to act increasingly as a channel for the Master to work through. Finally, a complete merger of energies occurs as the disciple becomes Self-realized as the ego boundaries dissolve. The fundamental principle is that the entire progress is dependent on the faith the disciple places in the Master. It is faith that keeps the channel open. It is faith that draws the connection closer, and it is increasing faith that allows it to expand. Without faith, no progress is possible.

And then there is the role of doubt. Doubts are the tests given to measure the strength and depth of the disciples' faith. They will occur from time to time to test the strength of the bond. If the disciple allows doubts to enter into the relationship, there is little the Master can do. Doubts are the worms that chew away at the energetic connection. Once established, they will gnaw holes through which the connective energy starts leaking away, and the energetic connection weakens. Once the first doubt has done its work, a second one finds it easier to enter, and over time, holes open up in the energy channel. Then the channel loses its ability to maintain an energetic connection between disciple and Master.

Faith

Therefore the disciple needs to be vigilant and robust because doubts may enter innocuously. It may be a remark from a family, relative, or friend, a passage in an article, a whispered rumour or slander that gives credibility, etc. All serve to test the mettle of the devotee. Is there sufficient faith to allow for a closer connection? This testing happens all the time. Once doubts are permitted to enter and are entertained by the mind, the relationship becomes broken sooner or later. The disciple loses a God-given opportunity for Self-realization in that lifetime.

It may take many lifetimes to receive another chance to connect with a *Satguru*, and every time the tests will reoccur. Once broken by lack of faith, the connection is tested repeatedly until finally, one develops a strong enough connection to withstand all attacks and allows the devotee to complete the journey. Merger with the *Satguru* energies can then occur, which is the same as merging with the Absolute.

An interesting illustration of the power of faith is that the devotees on the Soul Travel Path I initially travelled had inner experiences with spiritual Masters whose existence, as was later shown, were fabricated, having had no Earth history. Yet, a connection was formed on the inner planes through the faith of the devotees, which allowed Divine Spirit to use the Master's matrix to function as a spiritual connection through which teachings and protection could flow. It was faith that initiated the relationship and trust that maintained it.

In the words of Mohanji:

> *"Life is about faith. Faith happens, sooner or later. When ego subsides and gets nullified through consistent downfalls, faith happens. Faith leads. Faith soothes. Faith reinforces. Faith nurtures life. Faith elevates life. Faith stabilizes life. Faith liberates man. Faith increases with experiences. Faith decreases when we disown our own experiences; swapping it for other's opinions or book knowledge. Faith increases when surrender becomes absolute. Faith decreases when ego becomes predominant. Faith is real if it is spontaneous. Faith is transitory if it is induced or inherited. If man's herd instinct leads to a certain faith, it ends when he turns a new corner. Such is the passing faith, which has no longevity. Faith-based conviction is more real if the conviction is based on truth."*

Thank you, dear Master, for taking me home. I place my faith in you. Jai Mohanji!

"Faith can take us to the highest. Complete faith and perfect surrender to the satguru, making Him the main object of worship, obeying his words to its fullest, disciples can cut out the weeds of uncertainty and attain supreme bliss. Faith, Surrender and Patience mature a disciple and help his elevation. The Guru takes care of his well-being."

Mohanji

Mohanji & Hein Adamson

PATH OF PATHLESSNESS

Hein Adamson, South Africa
September 2014

The way a Guru operates is baffling and cannot be understood by the human mind. Hein shares a few learnings that he witnessed during his stay with Mohanji. He realised that Mohanji is a mirror filled with unconditional love and clarity of purpose. Only those who have the eyes can catch a glimpse of the ways of a Guru!

I first met Mohanji three years ago, and in that time I have learnt a lot and seen a lot. I have had the privilege of seeing my *Guru* in different contexts and situations, and I have spent close, intimate time with him for extended periods. Mohanji's Path, the Path of Shiva, the Path of Pathlessness, is both challenging and at the same time effortless, simple and yet mysterious, plain yet indescribably beautiful. This writing aims to share things I have learned and seen to share some of the pitfalls and glories of the journey thus far.

The love unconditional and the love relentless

One of the things that drew me to Mohanji is that he lives with what he teaches. He embodies and exemplifies his teachings and the fundamental teaching, the base of his tradition, is unconditional love. I have never seen or experienced anyone who expresses that as explicitly as he does. I have seen him spending hour after hour, day after day concerned for an individual half a world away. He will not rest until he has made every conceivable effort to bring some relief and solace to the one who is suffering, who is lonely, who needs a helping hand or who needs to feel that someone cares.

Of course, we are free, and we often choose to suffer as I have chosen many times. But Mohanji never lets us go, he walks with us every step of the way, in my case, every need is being taken care of and provided for by my *Guru*, from the totally mundane like food and shelter to the sublime like purpose, elevation and belonging.

I have often disregarded his guidance and his teachings to fall flat on my face and come crawling back to his feet; time after time without fail, he welcomes me with open arms. Many people have said negative things about me to Mohanji, to the effect that he is wasting his time on a host of other discouraging things and me, but he never sways; he has remained objective and pulled me up inch by inch. I have nothing to offer; I have no skills which could be exploited and no money from which he might profit; it's all love and only love.

I am not the only one, either. I know of a few cases where he personally sponsored seekers and devotees to enable them to travel with him, join him on a retreat or take a pilgrimage with him. There is zero expectation of return from anyone. It goes even further than that: many people who have been on the receiving end of gifts from Mohanji, who have had life-transforming experiences in his presence, have, in the height of ingratitude, betrayed these gifts and gone so far as to spread the most blatant and brazen falsehoods about him. Despite this, he remains unaffected, and his love remains undiminished. No one is ever rejected; no one's welcome is ever worn out. Once you are a part of Mohanji's family, you will never be without family again.

The Master and the mirror

He has no agenda whatsoever, outside of delivering to the person in front of him according to their eligibility. He never worries about the future, he never worries about the next year or the next day or the next hour, he flows from one moment to another with grace and elegance, seldom seen in this world. I have travelled with him for 27 uninterrupted days, spending nigh on 24 hrs of the day with him, long enough to know that this is genuine and cannot be a pretence; no one could maintain that level of grace and flexibility for that long if it weren't real.

There have been scientific experiments conducted on Mohanji which evince that he has essentially no mental activity. I once asked him whether he ever meditates, and he replied as follows: **"I have no mind, what will I meditate on?"** There have been occasions when I am contemplating on Mohanji, trying to understand better who and what he is and concluded that there is no such thing as Mohanji.

What we see when we look at Mohanji is nothing more or less than a reflection of ourselves. He is a perfect mirror, empty, pure and objective. The Masters all share this quality of emptiness and reflection; they become the person in front of them. When I came to him with doubt, he reflected doubt, when I came to him with anger, he reflected anger, and when I came to him with love, he reflected love. I have seen this time and again with many people who have come in contact with him. He always says that his job is to guide us to ourselves, to reveal ourselves. I often think of Mohanji and become very uncomfortable, I have to wonder, at those times, why am I feeling this way when he represents love and liberation? Contemplating thus, I inevitably come to the point where I realise that I am not uncomfortable at all; it is the "devil in me" that becomes restless. But what is it? What is the devil in me? That's an easy question to answer: It is my mind.

The infinite and the mind

For the vast majority of us, the only operating platform we have ever known is the mind. The mind through which we perceive the world is little more than a bundle of impressions and conditioning; it is a garbage bag where we keep all of our baggage and our junk.

Mohanji and the rest of the enlightened Masters throughout history have always been without this garbage bag. They operate not from the mental plane but from the plane of consciousness, which has no boundary and no limit. This, I think, is why we find it so difficult to understand them.

We try with limited faculties to understand the unlimited; we try to understand divine expressions using terrestrial means. Try as you might, you will not succeed. I have tried my entire life, over and over again to grasp the consciousness that Mohanji represents, to fit it into some sort of neat criteria or frame, to give it some sort of identity, but it is too alive to be put into a box that way. Just when I think I know what he is about, he frustrates my conclusion by expressing something else. The fault, I have realised, lies not with him but with me. He is available, accessible, and near, but to access Mohanji you have to become Mohanji and to become Mohanji, Hein must cease to be, he has to die his natural death every day.

The spontaneous and the liberated

I have never known Mohanji to be contrived in any way, nor have I known him to plan anything beforehand. Everything happens now, expressions happen now, giving happens now, liberation happens now. This moment is his only reality; he completes what can be completed now and leaves nothing half-finished with the idea that he can do it later. Whatever comes his way is accepted fully, he offers no resistance to any development or situation, nor does he hold on to any emotions. I have seen him put on a show of anger for the sake of a seeker; he will blow up entirely and then be laughing the very next moment. He is not bound or enslaved by these expressions. He remains detached.

There was at one point going to be an *ashram* in India which fell through. At a time when he existed basically as a nomad with no base and really no rest, a place to settle would have been a welcome relief. But even though it did not work out, he went about his business as though nothing had happened. He has faced revilement, jealousy, rejection and open enmity but continues to flow and to love unconditionally no matter the circumstance.

The purpose and the mission

Mohanji is the most intense and productive person I have ever met. There is literally not a moment which passes him by without being utilised. He sleeps very little, sometimes as little as 3 hours a night for a few nights in a row and even then is busy functioning and carrying out his mission on other planes and dimensions. Every breath he takes, every movement is loaded with clarity and purpose. He is totally and completely purpose-driven, 24 hours of the day, without stint, without interruption.

He is always travelling on a terrestrial level, going from one program to the next, delivering clarity and elevation through his discourses and meditations, which are always free of charge. He delivers subtle experiences to many people across the world in the various time zones on other levels. Sometimes he fights battles on astral and other levels for the sake of his devotees, the signs of which are visible even on his physical body. He often gets ill from absorbing and churning the karmic baggage and negativities of the people he comes in contact with. He never brings any attention to the subtle work he does, and stoically takes everything in his stride.

The purpose is so simple: liberation; liberation from habit, from limited patterns and from conditional thinking. In short: liberation form anything and everything which could bind us in any way.

The tragedy and the betrayal

When the truth confronts you, you have two options: heed the voice of truth, take the opportunity to release your conditioning and preconceived notions, to transform, to liberate yourself. Or, kill the one who speaks the truth, scandalise him (as in the case of Sai Baba, Mata Amritanada Mayi and Bhagawan Nithyananda), crucify him (as in the case of Jesus) or poison him (as in the case of Socrates and Osho). In short, to shut him/her up as quickly as possible and get him to stop saying things which might require me to re-evaluate my life and my priorities.

This message is in part an appeal to anyone who might come in contact with a Living Master, be it Mohanji or any other:

1. Let go of your limitations; let go of your ideas about what a saint should or should not be.

2. Drink up his presence and his gifts with humility and gratitude.

3. Above all, do not miss the opportunity they represent.

We never know how long it will be before another true Master comes to us; it could take many lifetimes before we again attain the eligibility required to benefit from an enlightened presence.

There is, to my mind, no greater tragedy than to miss this chance. I know very little, but I do know that once you have surrendered to someone like Mohanji, to a true *Guru*, everything in your life happens for one reason only: liberation. It does not matter how the *Guru* expresses himself, what he says or what he does, his purpose is to set you free, and your purpose is to let him do it.

The family and the unity

I have seen and heard about Mohanji coming into contact with many great Saints and Masters, both living and not. Through Mohanji, many have experienced Jesus, Mahavatar Babaji, Sai Baba and Gorakh Baba to name but a few. On a terrestrial level, any Master who meets Mohanji or Mohanji's devotees has always shown love and affection. Masters like Vittal Babaji, Devi Amma from Whitefield in Bangalore, Baba Nataraja in America, and Swami Chaitanyananda, entrusted with caring for Vasishta's sacred cave, and Gorakh Guruji in India have all welcomed Mohanji with love and openness. We are one family; we are one soul. The golden tradition of liberation and love is everywhere. That is what Mohanji represents, and that is what he makes available to us by his presence in our lives.

The path and the destination

I am ignorant and will not go into much detail about the Path of Pathlessness's depths. I will only say that here, there are no rules. Nothing is forbidden, and nothing is seen as wrong, nothing is ever expected of you. All you need to do is be natural and stay connected to the *Guru*'s consciousness. That is the only practice you need. Elevation, experience and knowledge are all provided by the Master. Surrender and faith are the only prerequisites. Grace is all you need, and grace is showered in abundance.

For me, Mohanji is both means and destination. I don't know about God or enlightenment, but I know that Mohanji can deliver me into the lap of the supreme. Whether I can understand it or not, whether it tallies with my limited notions or not, whether I find it pleasant or not, whatever he gives is absolutely in my best interest.

My eternal love and gratitude go to Mohanji now and ever!!

"I have always called you for generations. How come you never heard my call? I tried to wake you up many times, but you chose to sleep. I bring light to you. Choosing light or darkness is your discretion."

Mohanji

Mohanji & Jayashree Mukund Shinde

GURU SHIKHAR

Jayashree Mukund Shinde, USA

January 2021

Only when beckoned, can a seeker even attempt to climb the mighty Girnar and have the darshan of Lord Datta's footprints atop the hill. Jayashree's deep yearning became a reality as she succeeded in climbing the magnanimous mountain of 9999 steps. This was possible only by the grace and loving guidance of Mohanji, who was with her throughout this arduous journey!

Surrendering at the lotus feet of Lord Datta, also known as "Girnar Raja" – the king of the Mountain Girnar, I am beginning my story of 'Journey to Girnar with Mohanji'.

More ancient than the Himalayas is Mount Girnar – the mountain that symbolizes 'a *Guru* is always on top of the world.' Lord Dattatreya, the *Adi Guru* of Dattatreya Tradition, is believed to have meditated at the peak of this mountain for over 12,000 years.

Many devotees of Lord Datta climb up Mount Girnar throughout the year to get a glimpse of the benevolent *Guru*, Dattatreya. It is said that to reach the peak of the mountain and to have the *darshan* of his (Lord Dattatreya) holy footprints, one should have a lot of determination, dedication, surrender, and utmost faith. One should follow the same path as his *Guru,* in the same direction, and only then can he reach the destination. Lord Dattatreya is present here protecting all his devotees.

I had travelled to India in Jan 2020 to attend a retreat with Mohanji, spend some time with my parents, and attend a cousin's wedding. I would be in India for some more time, and while I was there, I tried to spend as much time as I could, being around Mohanji. In late January 2020, the *Bhumi Puja* of the 'Home for Seniors' land was happening in Thiruvannamalai, and I was so fortunate to attend the ceremony and to be able to meet Mohanji there.

A few days after returning from Thiruvannamalai, I heard about a short trip that Mohanji was making to Mount Girnar to Lord Datta's temple. I had not heard about this mountain and Lord Datta's temple before. I had no idea what it takes to go there! But, as soon as I heard about it, a calling from my heart came to travel with Mohanji to Mount Girnar. A wet blanket was soon thrown over my excitement when I heard that going to Lord Datta's temple on top of the mountain means climbing up 9999 steps and down the same too!

I shivered with the reality check. I didn't think I could do this as I am not very fit physically. I gave up the idea. That's when I got a message from Rajesh saying "You are coming to Girnar. *Jo Dar Gaya Samjho Woh Mar Gaya.*" (The one who is scared, is dead). His words were motivating enough, and I felt as if these words were coming from Mohanji! So, I decided to take the journey! On top of that, Rajesh assured me about the possibility of using the *doli* service, where you can be carried up rather than walk. I decided I would go to Girnar and take a *doli*.

I reached Junagadh in the afternoon of February 11th. Several people from Mohanji family had already arrived there, and I was taken to the beautiful Gorakhnath Ashram overlooking Mount Girnar. After lunch, Ruchika and I went around feeding cows around the Gorakhnath Ashram. Later, after Mohanji arrived, all of us gathered in his room. Mohanji was very happy to see all of us. I noticed that Mohanji's left foot's swelling had not reduced (which was there since the Thiruvannamalai event). Seeing all of us worrying about his foot pain, Mohanji very lovingly told us, "You are all Mai-Tri Practitioners. So why don't you do Mai-Tri to this body? To the body only, not to Mohanji!" It's beyond our imagination to heal Mohanji's body, but we realized that to keep our worrying mind at rest, Mohanji gave us this opportunity. In my heart, I was praying to Datta to relieve this physical pain from Mohanji's foot.

We had a small *satsang* with Mohanji about Girnar and the plan to climb in the night to reach the top by early morning for *aarati* at 5:30 am. Rajesh Kamath mentioned that I wanted to take a *doli* as it was difficult for me to climb. Mohanji immediately said, **"Shinde has to climb, she will climb, it's her *sadhana*"**. This was a command from my *Guru*, and I bowed down to this and said, "Yes *Baba*, all your grace, your will".

As Mohanji reminded us all, "A visit to Girnar is not an ordinary journey. It is a surrender and commitment to the Tradition. Unless you have deep commitment and conviction, you may not be in this land. In fact, there is no better place, more powerful and more relevant than Girnar for a true spiritualist in the path of the *Avadhootas* (total dissolution). We aren't talking about enlightenment or even the Path of the *Siddhas* here – this is much beyond human realms or thinking. Even today, the nine *Naths* and 84 *Siddhas* visit Girnar in *sookshma* form, chant and pray for the *darshan* of Lord Dattatreya who continues to guide them. Grace alone can bring an individual to this land. Grace and surrender alone will help one complete this holy pilgrimage. Jai Gurudev Datta!"

After the empowering *satsang* with Mohanji, we got ready to start our climb to Mount Girnar. Along with me, Ruchika, Sonia, Hemkant and his wife Shilpa were ready too. After attending the *aarati* at Gorakhnath temple and dinner, we started our walk around 9 pm. We took blessings from Lord

Datta and Hanuman's idols at the bottom of Girnar and started climbing from there.

We had no idea about what the climbing path would be like, or how long it will take. We all carried a stick, a bottle of water, and chanting Lord Datta's name, we kept on climbing. As we picked up our pace, a couple of people fell behind. As I was walking, I felt that there were Masters from above looking at us. I could feel their energy around us.

Walking up the steep steps wasn't easy for me. My knees hurt, and my legs felt weak to move. I had to take frequent stops to sit down and then kept on walking. At some point, all of us met up again, and we sat down at that point to meditate for a few minutes and then continued walking. While we were walking, an elderly couple joined us. I spoke to them about Mohanji, Mohanji's mission, liberation and gave a brief of his teachings, too.

At some point during our walk, we noticed that George had arrived. He was walking very fast, chanting "Jai Gurudeva Datta, Hari Om Tat-Sat" loudly. When he saw us, he hugged us and kept on walking. Seeing the energetic George walking with such speed, chanting loudly, I felt a sudden surge of energy in my own body. He reminded me of Lord Hanuman, who was empowered because of his faith and devotion. Hemkant started walking fast, ahead with George. The rest of us were walking at our own pace, Shilpa and I were together, walking, talking, and resting. It was not so easy, and the body would give up. In those moments, I thought of Mohanji and Lord Datta and reminded myself that this is my path; this is my destination; this is the goal – to reach Datta, I have to do it.

Surrendering each step to Lord Datta, I kept walking. Something in me started telling me, "keep walking." Slowly, the energy started flowing, and I could climb with lesser effort.

After some time, I saw that Hemkant was resting because of severe pain in his knee, and Shilpa was with him. George went ahead. I could not wait with Hemkant because the inner voice said, "keep walking". I kept walking, and another old couple was walking along too. We sent a balm for Hemkant that the couple had with them through some people going down, and we kept on walking ahead.

After 3000 steps, we reached the Neminath Tirthankar temple along with the elderly couple.

Following a brief rest, I started climbing up again alone. It was pitch dark. I had no torch. The couple were still resting behind, but I kept walking even in the darkness. I could feel the pull of some divine energy which was making me walk. I didn't know the path, but I kept on walking. When I felt tired, I would feel a sudden surge of energy as soon as I surrendered to Mohanji and Dattatreya.

After a while, I heard Mohanji and his group coming behind us, Mohanji in a *doli*. I looked back at them, and I wanted to go towards Mohanji. Mohanji saw me and said, **"Shinde don't come back, keep walking, and go ahead"**. Now, I was walking with even more energy and joy, knowing that Mohanji and the group are walking just behind me. I had no more fear, no more pain; I started climbing higher and higher. With each step, I was surrendering and climbing.

It was dark everywhere and pin-drop silence. Not a single soul to be seen. I was just taking each step slowly and going up with complete faith. After the 5000th step, I reached Ambaji's temple. The doors of the temple were closed, and I did not know what to do. Mohanji's words "keep walking" were always ringing in my head. So, I got up from the temple and started climbing again. Through ups and downs, amidst the dark in the silent path, walking continuously, finally I reached the Gorakhnath temple at around 7000 steps.

At this point, the only sound was the sound of the wind blowing; hard-hitting, strong and cold. I also knew there were wild animals in those mountains, which I could not see or hear. I felt the presence of some Masters above me, walking along with me. It was not that I was walking alone. Datta *Guru* Mohanji was watching over me and that was the reason for this huge surge of energy coursing through my body, making me walk. I remembered only these two things while walking.

At one point, the steps go down, and then they take off to go to the ultimate, Guru Shikhar – the peak. Climbing these steep steps towards the peak, I suddenly felt there were no thoughts. There was only emptiness. I had only two thoughts in my mind, to reach Guru Shikhar and be at the Datta temple before the *aarati* and to keep walking.

I was walking like a daredevil, without any fear of the solitude or darkness. Suddenly at one point, my stick slipped from my hand and went down somewhere in the dark. It can be quite a discomfort being without a stick in the darkness. I started chanting and climbing down slowly. Maybe after 50 steps or so, I saw my stick! It was stuck to something, and I had spotted it even in the dark. I picked up the stick, thanked Mohanji and Datta and started walking again with focus. At times, the fear of walking alone came to mind, but at those times, I felt the Masters watching over me and Mohanji's presence with me, protecting me. My fear vanished with this understanding. I remembered Mohanji's words, "keep walking" and so I kept walking.

The final part of climbing was very steep, but I didn't even realize how I climbed that part. Finally, I saw a flag and the top of Guru Shikhar, the top of the temple and I started climbing further. It was getting even windier at the top, and I felt that I might fall.

Guru Shikhar

After climbing carefully, I reached the top, and I saw George sitting just below the Datta temple. He guided me to go further up near the temple, and when I arrived there, I saw Rajesh Kamath and DB. It was 4 am (*Brahma Muhurtha*) when I reached the Datta temple.

I walked up and touched the temple; now was the time to sit down! At that point, I had an immense surge of energy in me, and I wasn't feeling cold or wind beat. Rajesh forced me to wear my jacket and then I sat down. It was as if Mohanji acted like my Mother, making sure I was protected from the cold wind. As soon as I put on my jacket and sat, intense pain started in my stomach centre near the navel, going back to my spine, like some pull, it was very painful. I didn't know what it was and I started crying out to Datta. Rajesh helped me lie down and to rest completely, and soon I felt better. Datta's healing energy had taken my pain away in minutes!

After about half an hour, Mohanji and the rest of the group arrived too. As soon as Mohanji saw me, he said, "Ah, Shinde, you are already there". I said "*Baba*, all your love and grace" and I bowed down to him.

We were waiting for the temple to open at 5:30 am for the *aarati*. While the slight delay was happening, Sonia and Ruchika arrived. Then after the temple opened, while we were going inside, Hemkant and Shilpa arrived too. The entire Mohanji family was inside the temple just in time for the *aarati*. Mohanji ensured that everyone was there together with him. This was the great divine grace of Datta.

Just before the *aarati*, while I was standing behind Mohanji, he said to Ananth who was there in the front, **"You know this Shinde, she can talk about liberation in three minutes"**. I blushed because I realized that Mohanji heard my conversation with the couple while walking about our Tradition, Masters, liberation etc. Mohanji reminded me once again that he is always listening to us.

Soon *aarati* started. It was such a powerful and divine moment to attend the Datta *aarati* in the physical presence of Mohanji. I couldn't believe myself; I was physically there receiving this grace!!! I was speechless, completely merged with the divine grace of Mohanji and Datta. Time had stopped for me at that moment. So far, it was one of the greatest moments of my life.

After *aarati*, we went around the Lord Dattatreya's idol inside the temple, had a good *darshan* and came out. After the 7-8 hours long sadhana of climbing up, the descent was joyful. Yes, Mohanji ensured that the descent was joyous. Sonia, Ruchika and I started climbing down together, talking laughing, eating, our legs were flying with joy! Such satisfaction, such contentment!

Guru Shikhar

We had many interesting incidents during our walk down, like meeting some strange people. We went to Gorakhnath temple and heard the priest's inspiring story there who had left his banker job to serve in the temple. We then reached the Ambaji temple where we had *darshan* of the divine Mother and finally decided to sit down for some time to take rest. We were feeling as if we were flying, and we felt so light. We laughed at small things.

On our way down, we met an older man looking like a *yogi*. He told us so many stories of Mount Girnar. We kept walking down, enjoying our journey together. After a while, we saw some monkeys and gave them watermelon. Then, from nowhere, a person started walking with us even after we said we didn't need any help; he just wanted to accompany us. In between an old mother wanted some food for her children and we bought some food for her. Finally, in the mix of laughing, sitting, and walking, we reached the bottom of Mount Girnar and arrived at the Gorakhnath ashram. We offered food and some money to the person who had been walking with us all this time.

The next day, before leaving Girnar, we met Mohanji to express our gratitude and take his blessings. Again, Mohanji said to me, "Why do you need a *doli*, when you have this body?" He explained to me what a beautiful gift we have as this body and its importance. I was in deep gratitude, and tears rolled down my cheeks. Everything that happened the day before was only by the grace of my Datta, *Guru* Mohanji.

After returning from Girnar, I felt Mohanji was Lord Datta and daily did the Swami Samarth Datta *aarati*. However, Mohanji fulfilled every desire of mine within a few days. Mahesh Bhalero sang a new Girnar Datta *aarati* to Mohanji. I was overjoyed, and now I do the Mohanji Datta *aarati* every day.

On my return to Bangalore, I also visited Devi Amma to give her Ganga water from Varanasi and some Tamil books and spoke about the Girnar trip with Mohanji. Devi Amma said, "You have shed many lifetimes karmic baggage by climbing Girnar with Mohanji." Then I understood what Mohanji had meant when he said, "It's your *sadhana*." It meant shedding karmic baggage.

Visiting Girnar had not been on my bucket list. Not even a thought had been there, at least not in my conscious mind. But it all just happened with the grace of Datta and the miracle of my *Guru* Mohanji. Even today, when I look back, I get goose bumps. How did it happen?

The truth is that the journey to Girnar happens only with complete faith and devotion, the grace of Dattatreya, and Datta *Guru* Mohanji, who carries you ahead.

Guru Shikhar

This *yatra* (pilgrimage) to Girnar with Mohanji will remain close to my heart forever.

At the lotus feet of Gurudeva Datta Mohanji!

Jai Gurudev Datta. Guru Mohanaya Namaha.

Mohanji & Madhusudan Rajagopalan

CALM AMIDST THE STORM

Madhusudan Rajagopalan, India
February 2021

In this beautiful experience, Madhu highlights the practical and subtle ways a Guru operates, showering the followers with grace and protection. This can be seen and felt only when one cares to see. Madhu speaks about how Mohanji took a large group of people to safety during a devastating flood in a South Indian city!

After a fantastic trip to Tiruvannamalai in November 2015, we travelled to Chennai for the trip's final leg. A public *Satsang* was scheduled the next day (24th Nov 2015), probably the first gathering in Chennai in many years. As a native of Chennai and the coordinator for the whole program, I led our group's logistics.

Our last day in Tiruvannamalai was action-packed, to put it mildly. A few of us started early at 3 am for the *Girivalam* (circumambulation of the holy mountain of Arunachala). Once we returned to our hotel, Mohanji joined the whole group to visit the temple (Lord Annamalaiyar, i.e. Lord Shiva) for a *darshan*. There were already signs of inclement weather as Mohanji would often rush us to move, pointing at the skies. We then visited the *samadhi* shrines of the great saints, Seshadri Swamigal, Ramana Maharishi and finally the *ashram* of Yogi Ramsuratkumar. We were privileged to spend some time with Ma Devaki, one of Yogiji's closest disciples and the *ashram*'s chief caretaker. Ma Devaki arranged for us to have *prasad* at the *ashram* and we eventually returned to our hotel around 3 pm.

Initially, we had planned to leave around 1 pm and reach Chennai for a late evening dinner so that Mohanji could rest the next morning, and we could prepare for the *Satsang* that evening.

However, we could leave only around 4 pm, after the final packing and check-out formalities. We were about 15 people, in 2 vehicles – an Innova car with Mohanji and a few people, plus a minibus with the rest of the group. When we stopped to fill fuel in the vehicles, the drivers realised that they would need to cover the minibus's top with tarpaulin sheets to protect our luggage from the rains. This took another 20-30 minutes. We were already delayed, and this hold-up was playing on my frayed nerves. However, I knew this was essential with the prevailing weather – a test of acceptance for me right then!

As we finally set out for Chennai, we were mentally prepared for a long journey and hoped to reach home late in the night. During the journey, we were getting regular updates from our families in Chennai about the rain situation. Normally, Chennai gets light rainfall. However, on this day, it seemed like the clouds were emptying themselves into Chennai! Every half hour, we would get an update that the rain was non-stop and getting heavier.

Around 6.15 pm, Mohanji called me from his car, asking us to find a good place for an early dinner. Soon, we found a food court area on the highway. Mohanji insisted that everyone should eat well, use the toilet facilities and refresh themselves so that the whole group, including our drivers, was comfortable. Our group didn't need much encouragement to eat tasty *dosas* and *idlis*, but the instructions from Mohanji came as a welcome break from the hectic schedule since morning; everyone complied happily! We had three children in the group as well, and they got a chance to move around and beat the tedium of the journey.

We resumed our journey after the dinner break, and by 8.30 pm, we reached a suburb that is 20 km from the Chennai airport. From there, normally, it would take less than an hour to the airport, even in rush hour traffic. But that evening, we hit massive traffic and literally inched ahead. Two hours later, we were still nowhere near the airport. We were getting reports that the rain was still as heavy and that the city roads were flooded with many cars stranded.

My phone battery was also running low. Thankfully, I was able to borrow a power bank, and that allowed me to stay functional on the phone. I was in the minibus' front seat, next to the driver and mentally willing the vehicle forward. People's edges were beginning to fray slowly, not to mention the driver's growing fatigue and anxiety. Nonetheless, we were in the mood to soldier through and get home somehow, as we were just around 12 km from home by then.

Around that time, Mohanji called me. In his usual, brisk manner, he said: "Let us look for some hotels near the airport; it doesn't look like we can go into the city tonight." I said OK and reluctantly began searching for options. One part of my brain was protesting - "This is Chennai, my hometown, I know the place and how far we are from home. Why can't we push through and reach home? It would be weird to stay in a hotel in the same city where my parents and my in-laws live. Who does that?"

Another part of my brain was going "Well, Mohanji gave you instructions, just follow it!" In any case, I found a few Oyo listed hotels from a quick internet search. To my surprise, many hotels were already booked out. Finally, we found one hotel which had the requisite number of rooms to fit our group. I made reservations and told the front desk executive that we would be reaching soon.

Reaching this hotel required us to turn right from the highway into a small lane, soon after crossing the airport. As we were making our way there, we missed the right turn. The next turn required us to go through an underpass; unfortunately, this had become a lake by then, thanks to the heavy rains. We turned around with no other option and tried to locate the correct turn (a left turn, now that we had turned around) to the hotel. As we were slowly driving back, looking for the turn, we crossed the airport. I realised then that we had missed the route to the hotel altogether. I was supposedly the "navigator", clearly not a very good one!

In my head, I was playing out scenarios of how I would answer Mohanji and sweating! While my heart was still racing fast, we noticed one other Oyo hotel. The time was well past 11.30 pm by now, and thankfully, the rains had taken a small break, so I could walk across to the hotel to check on availability. The hotel was quite basic, but most importantly, he had just enough free rooms to hold us (7 rooms for the 15 of us), the rooms looked clean, and the tariffs were reasonable (no price gouging in an emergency!). Plus, we saw some other airport passengers at the front desk, which gave us some comfort. We quickly confirmed our rooms for the night and arranged for our vehicles to bring the group to the hotel.

Though we had found a hotel, I couldn't help feeling a sense of guilt for having put the group through difficulty. Our group had finished a full retreat in Kumbakonam and a pilgrimage in Tiruvannamalai; instead of reaching home for some rest, we were stranded in a small hotel near the Chennai airport. I saw Mohanji standing outside the hotel as he was waiting for the group to go in. I approached him and apologised for all the trouble we were putting him and the group through. **He calmly replied, "Don't worry. Big problems are solved this way. Just be practical and keep moving".** I didn't fully grasp what that meant, but his words made me feel lighter, and I carried on with the rest of the arrangements.

We had to look after the group's requirements – water, snacks and some necessary medicines for any emergencies. The hotel didn't have any of this, and we had to arrange for this post-midnight. Even under normal circumstances, shops in Chennai don't stay open this late. On a rain-battered day like this, that seemed like a more significant challenge.

In any case, Rajesh (Kamath) and I decided to drive around to check. As luck would have it, we found a 24-hour medical shop within a few minutes. We quickly bought crates of water bottles, snacks (biscuits, potato chips etc.) and some medicines and returned to the hotel. Things working out like this in Chennai were surely a sign of grace – imagine our situation if no shops had been open or if the weather was worse; we would have had hotel rooms but nothing more!

We informed our families that we were staying at this hotel and settled in well after 1.30 am. We were grateful that we had beds to sleep in and were not stuck on the road or in flooded vehicles. After the blissful stay in Kumbakonam (in a classy, heritage property) and in Tiruvannamalai, this hotel seemed like a big downgrade in quality. Though, at that point in time, I think people were past the point of caring – just a clean bed and not having to be cooped up in a vehicle seemed like a divine blessing! Just goes to show how our mind over-complicates the simple needs of life and builds walls or concepts that take us away from what really matters!

It had been a very long and eventful day; for some of us who had woken up at 2:30 am for the *Girivalam*, it had literally been 24 hours of non-stop action and movement. Though it didn't feel like that for many of us - when Mohanji's energy is fuelling action, there is no question of fatigue, and one just keeps moving! I believe most of the group had a sound sleep that night.

The next morning, we woke up to phone calls that told us about several horror stories. People had been forced to abandon their cars on the road; arterial roads had become rivers, several houses and areas were flooded, and there was pandemonium throughout the city. It was then that we realised what we had escaped! If we had gone ahead yesterday without stopping at the hotel, we would have definitely been stuck on the road with no way to get to any safe place. Imagine a group of 15 people in 2 different vehicles, including foreigners, children and tons of luggage - it would have been a nightmare of the worst kind!

We understood what Mohanji meant when he said, "Big problems are solved in this way". We grasped that a big calamity had been reduced to minor discomforts – some physical, i.e. the arduous journey, an unplanned stay at a 1star hotel, and some mental, i.e. the sheer uncertainty of what would come next, worries about how we would manage etc. While going through the experience, it felt like a big discomfort. But what may have been in store for us would have been much worse.

As more information trickled in, we learnt that was among the heaviest 24-hour spells (~139mm) of rainfall in Chennai. People were sharing stories of how vehicles were submerged; people stuck in traffic for hours together in the dead of night, homes flooded, etc.

When I think about how grace had a role to play in the events of that evening, two things really stood out. During this whole episode, Mohanji gave just two instructions –

1. He asked us to have an early dinner. Most of us were mentally prepared for dinner after 8 pm, given our late lunch. When one leaves late, one wants to make up for the time and

cover the maximum distance before it gets too dark. However, his counter-intuitive instruction ensured that everyone was well fed well in time, and nobody got cranky despite inordinate delays. Amazingly, even the children were models of cooperation through the journey!

2. He told us to find a hotel near the airport instead of going home as per our original plan. For a native Chennaiite, that was quite hard to accept.

In both cases, the decision at that point seemed strange. But post facto, those were the decisions that saved us. The test here was all about flexibility and calm decision making. We had to adapt to the situation and act based on what was in front of us. There was no time to agonise over what could have been – e.g., why didn't we leave earlier, if only we had beaten the traffic by 30 minutes, if we could just get past that bottleneck and other such imaginary scenarios. None of that would have been of any use.

Breaking patterns is another aspect – staying in a hotel in my hometown was out of my frame of acceptable scenarios. Being compelled to consider that option taught me lessons in fluidity objectively. As Mohanji often says **"Be like water."** On that rainy day, the irony couldn't have been more hard-hitting!

In the morning, we managed to arrange tea for our group and the snacks that we had bought the previous night came in handy. We had asked people to rest as there was no tearing hurry in the morning until we worked out the rest of the transport arrangements. We still had to get home; we had a series of programs for the day and a *Satsang* with Mohanji later that evening!

Given the devastation, it was hardly any surprise that there were no vehicles available. A travel agent known to me agreed to send a 17-seater vehicle to enable our entire group to travel together. But within half an hour, he cancelled, citing vehicle damage due to heavy water-logging in the night. We then decided to call multiple taxis and send people in smaller groups. We contacted several taxi providers but had no luck until 10.30 am since the inclement weather had forced most vehicles off the roads.

Further, many roads were still severely flooded, which meant reduced mobility and greater risk of travel. Out of options, we asked our family to send their cars with the drivers. We decided to send Mohanji first to reach early and prepare for the day's engagements.

The morning was relatively pleasant with the rain gods taking a breather. As we waited for our cars to reach the hotel, some of us went downstairs and stepped outside. There was a non-descript store in front of the hotel selling various sheets and logs of wood. It had a mini-truck in front of the store. Someone suggested checking if we could hire the vehicle for transporting us to our destination. In any case, we had nothing to lose. All and sundry had already rejected us. One more hardly mattered!

To our surprise, the driver agreed immediately and that too at a reasonable price. A truly unexpected blessing of a vehicle calmly waiting right in front of us while we unsuccessfully moved heaven and earth to scour the entire city for one. Soon we had all our luggage loaded onto the mini-truck. With the entire luggage taken care of, even if the small cars had to shuttle up and down twice, we could take the whole group home within a few hours, without any other external dependency.

By the time we finished loading the mini-truck, our two cars had arrived. We decided that the mini truck would travel with the cars to guide the driver with directions. Rajesh volunteered to sit with the driver and save space for others in the cars. At that point, a few excited folks decided to jump onto the open back of the truck and make themselves comfortable on top of the luggage! As soon as this suggestion came up, the children, along with one lady from abroad, decided to join the party and hopped onto the open back of the mini truck.

Soon, this motley convoy of cars and truck left for our destination. The children had a fun time on the journey, looking back at Mohanji in the car and waving at all and sundry. They were a source of entertainment for the others on the road! Quite a friendly and jolly way to conclude an eventful journey. As Mohanji commented wryly, rain or floods, the M family would keep moving forward!

Meanwhile, one of the taxis turned up too, and the whole group reached home by around 1 pm for a sumptuous South Indian lunch. Following lunch, Mohanji continued working at his regular, fast pace to ensure no cancellations of programs scheduled in Chennai. We noticed how the weather held up in Chennai for as long as Mohanji was there. The previous day (23rd Nov) had seen crazy rains. That morning, before we left the hotel, Mohanji had commented that the rains would give us safe passage while we were in Chennai, but the rains would come back with greater force soon.

As it played out, that day in Chennai had a reasonable amount of sunshine. The next day (25th Nov) was fine too, and our group, including Mohanji, dispersed from Chennai. A few days later, the rains returned, and the first week of December 2015 saw the heaviest floods in Chennai in decades! The events of this trip served to confirm the subtlety of grace.

Grace is visible in the smallest of things if only one cares to see. This subtlety drives perfection. However, it takes faith and conviction. One has to follow the words of the Master without questioning, and things get taken care of on their own.

Painting By Mina Vlaketic

RESURRECTION OF LAZARUS

A Mohanji Follower
December 2019

Here is a miraculous escape from the jaws of death of a follower, saved only by the grace and protection of Mohanji! He had set out on this journey to the Himalayas with Mohanji's blessings and escaped unscathed after an accident! When faith and surrender to the Master are foremost, the unseen hand of protection is like an armour regardless of physical distance.

I died (well almost). And Mohanji brought me back to life.

Writing this anonymous account ensures that my family does not panic after reading the incident that I am about to narrate. Hence, it will obscure certain names of locations to protect me and my companion's identity.

In India, Diwali is a big festival and is accompanied by holidays at work. I decided to put the few days of Diwali holidays to good use by going to the Himalayas and doing some serious spiritual practices. I consulted Mohanji, and he told me about the practices that needed to be done.

The place I was going to has a very powerful Goddess temple. I planned to drive all night so that I could reach it early in the morning. I was travelling with a companion who had fallen asleep while I negotiated the mountain roads in the dead of night.

As the car turned a corner, I saw a leopard crouched by the road. I stopped the car and woke up my companion to also look. We watched it for a few minutes until it leapt and disappeared in the hills. I didn't think much of it at that time, but should I have? Was it Divine Mother?

In the next few days, I did my spiritual practices intensely sitting on Divine Mother's lap.

On the way back, I stopped by the ashram of a very famous saint (who is no longer in the body) and known to be Lord Hanuman's incarnation. As I sat down before his seat, my third eye area immediately started to vibrate as if receiving a *Shaktipat*. After some time, we started again towards home, Mohanji's *padukas* and the *Sri Yantra* of Divine Mother in a shoulder bag strapped safely in the back seat, like how one would tuck in a small child, with the seat belt.

Within about half an hour, the accident happened. As the car was coming down the mountain road, the brakes failed, and the steering jammed, mysteriously. My companion and I knew that we were about to fall off the mountain when the brakes failed to stop the car. Suddenly, the car was off the road and tumbling down the mountainside, as they show in the movies. I vividly remember the alternating darkness and light as the car tumbled down while flipping.

People confess their surrender to God or Guru while they are hale and hearty. It is difficult to replicate the few seconds before death and one's reaction during those last seconds. I was dead calm. As the car was crashing down, I thought I would die, and I calmly took three names: Mohanji, *Maa* (meaning Divine Mother) and the name of the saint whose ashram I had just visited. The car came to a stop. (We later came to know that the vehicle had fallen about 100 feet!).

No frantic sentences were uttered while the car was crashing, nor did I see my life flashing before me. The airbags had saved both of us. We were bleeding a little from cuts here and there, but as we climbed out of the car, we realized that neither had any serious injuries. Miraculously within minutes, villagers arrived and rescued us.

As we climbed to the top of the mountain where we had gone off the road, villagers told us that a shoulder bag was found on the road. This was the same shoulder bag which contained Mohanji's *padukas* and Mother's *Sri Yantra*. It is as if they stepped out at the top of the mountain, anchored themselves and stopped the car from falling further!

We were later informed by the villagers that, the tree which stopped the car from falling further was the last tree on that mountainside. After that, there was a sheer drop of about a kilometre down the ragged mountain into the river below. Of course, we all realized what could have happened had the car fallen further.

It seemed as if Divine Mother and Mohanji fought with Yama, the God of Death, themselves to stop him from taking us away.

As I waited for the police to arrive, the only thought was that I knew for sure, the strong bond I have with my Guru, Mohanji – as I was about to die, I took his name. There was also a certain comfort and blissful feeling that my surrender and faith were tested and not found inadequate.

This reminds me of the beautiful Indian *bhajan* (spiritual song) which goes:

> ***Itna toh karna swami jab praana tan se nikle,***
> ***Govind naam lekar phir praana tan se nikle***

This means that – Lord, as my life exits from my body, please allow me to take your name.

Almost felt like James Bond – straightened my imaginary tie after climbing out of the crash! Why should I care, when 'M' has my back! (And no, I am not talking about 007's boss!)

Resurrection Of Lazarus

When surrender is complete at the lotus feet of the *Guru*, the *Guru* will cross the cosmos to protect you and hold your hand in a split of a second. Physical distances are meaningless between a *Guru* and the devotee. What truly matters is the bond between the hearts.

Over the next few days, we finally managed to reach home. Apart from the car, we did not suffer any other loss – physical harm (Can you imagine tumbling 100 feet down a rugged mountainside and not requiring even one stitch?), wallets, travel bags, among other things.

Incidentally, I had left *Shiva Kavach* and *Devi Kavach* mantras, recited by Mohanji, playing on a loop in my altar room at home. Was this a coincidence?

Mohanji has resurrected me many times before, from sure death, but those stories are for another time.

Today, Lazarus lives, saved by his Jesus.

Painting By Mina Vlaketic

MASTERING CRISES

Mohanji's Shadow
January 2014

Mohanji says, 'Doubts will happen but do not allow them to stay." This is precisely what this follower did. He was filled with so many doubts and disillusioned by religions, saints and spirituality. Watching Mohanji in close quarters changed all that, and he sought forgiveness from this great Master who walks the talk and leads by example.

Sri. Sri. Mohanji, my sincere apologies to you for doubting you, as I write this for the sake of spiritual seekers across the world. Perhaps those who understand my mind will find the right answers and happiness. Many of you may have experienced the same thoughts. Those who stay with the superficial can't be helped anyway.

Even now, I am surprised that I am writing this. I am generally a skeptical person. I am inspired by people like Ms. Sabrina, Mr. Zoran and Ms. Palak Mehta who are bold enough to share their intimate life and the transformation that happened to them in the presence of Mohanji using their name. I admit that many of us do not have your guts or conviction when it comes to faith. I often feel that

I am a pseudo spiritualist who only takes from everyone, and never gives. Many of the seekers of the world are like me. We live in a fake world with fake people. We are all here to take something from saints without wanting to give anything back to anyone. We are generally selfish people with a few exceptions.

I am a rational man and never quite believed in God at most times of my life. I never quite believed in spiritual people because I considered that the Godmen who live in or visit our Delhi area are either criminals in disguise or con-men to power brokers for politicians. I believe we are not exposed to real saints who need nothing from us or do not come to our part of the earth. Perhaps there are some real ones in isolated places. This is not about scriptural knowledge; this is about the true stature of the saint.

I have always been skeptical about the whole Hindu religious structure with its multiple gods, many rituals. I was deeply disturbed by the class divides based on the caste system within Hindu life, which I strongly believe is held intact by politicians for the sake of votes. When I was doing my engineering, I realized that in addition to hard work, if one wants to be successful career-wise in India, one has to be born into certain specific castes. In a way, this divide has still left a scar in my mind. I strongly hate discrimination. The worthy should be honoured.

Thus disturbed, I decided to explore Christianity. I became part of a Christian group. However, as I became regular with them, I saw the rich and the poor's clear apparent classes. The priests befriended me only for one reason – conversion. And I saw how they subtly manipulate our insecurities. Everyone approaching the places of worship is in some kind of trouble. They become fair game for conversion. They are either brought in by 'agents', whose deep display of benevolence is usually well appreciated by the depressed.

They are also deluded in believing they have reached heaven and will not be discriminated anymore. Soon, after conversion, they are no longer needed by anyone. To stay in favour, they must bring more people for conversion. I also understood that conversions were associated with headcounts and votes. Votes mean power. Position, power, manipulation - thus goes the story.

I believed that the Hindu system and Saints lack unity. Each saint isolates himself in self-created comfort zones, fighting wars with other saints. Thus, they maintain the class difference. After having seen it all, I decided that being neutral and aloof to this mad world of religion was the right way of life. Spirituality is certainly good. Religion is not. Religion only amounts to divisions. Thus I had stopped searching, and I was quite content with myself and all my deficiencies. Then one of my colleagues introduced me to the name Mohanji.

I spontaneously Googled and discovered he is reasonably famous abroad though little known in India. My first thought was that perhaps he lacked a PR company to support him!

When I first saw the picture of Mohanji, I was as usual quite skeptical. Another *Guru*! These guys are doing it for the money. *Guru*-dom is big business these days. During my college days, I had approached many *gurus* and had paid huge bills for some group courses that changed nothing inside! I was not the least bit interested in Mohanji because I was reasonably prejudiced about *Gurus* in general! Our media always makes it a point to scandalize Hindu gurus for political gains. Then, I happened to come across Mohanji's blog, 'The Path of Pathlessness'. I felt a lot of genuineness in his words, and I got many answers. The next blog I read was, 'The Power of Losing'. I also found that quite interesting and genuine, as we have been indoctrinated to win! Thus, I read more and more and gradually moved into the Mohanji Consciousness. After a few months of reading and digesting, I decided to attend his next program in Delhi. I waited. After a few months of waiting, he came. I attended his program. I was eager to hear him talk and interact. My mind still held some skepticism. I asked a few questions and his answers were straight and no-nonsense. In a way, I liked it. He was definitely not trying to impress. He seemed to have his own experiences from where he was deriving the knowledge. There was no quoting of scriptures, no blaming other religions, and there was no-nonsense. He just said everything in a matter of fact way and left the place without any ceremonies.

He seemed genuine. I chatted with one young lady clicking away at Mohanji with her camera, which he did not seem to notice, and asked her – What attracts you to Mohanji? She said, "He is genuine. He is fearless. He genuinely cares without expectations. He is totally unconditional." Later, as I chatted with another person, I learned much more about Mohanji than what we could glean from the blogs. He is married to a foreigner; he has a baby daughter, has a corporate job, earns his livelihood through work, and calls a spade a spade. He has even angered some of his close followers by telling them bitter truths about themselves or scolding them out of love. If he is bold and cares about truth more than a relationship, then he is genuine. I always loved people who were truthful and straight. If he is so truthful, then he is needed in today's world of pseudo-spirituality. The world needs Mohanji.

Thus, my first meeting with him from a distance became a good memory, and I developed the urge to be with him and associate with his movement. I found his team were mostly youngsters and they loved him as a father, brother, close friend with whom you can share anything and everything, or as a guide more than a guru. There was a sense of family-ship within Mohanji's group. No hierarchical feeling. Moreover, Mohanji is on social networks such as Facebook; he takes calls; he answers emails himself; he is available to people without fees or barriers. He has no inhibitions, fears or apparent taboos. He encourages people to do dharmic business and feed the poor. He is concerned about cruelty against animals. He is against female foeticide. I became more and more attracted to Mohanji and more than that, to his lifestyle. He seems to live his teachings. He seems to be active in business life, charity and spiritual life. He seems to have no inhibitions as seen from his pictures in various costumes and situations. A bandana and dark glasses for a *guru*! He has no frame, no image barrier! Good. Perhaps I have found my guide. I still wanted to take more time, though before addressing him as my *guru*. I was still not sure. Then, I heard most people calling him father in Delhi and that suited me too.

In November 2013, Mohanji's charity institution Ammucare conducted a concert in Delhi for Autism awareness. I felt inclined to support that in my own way because I found genuineness in the young team members' eyes. There was a deep love for Mohanji and the mission in their hearts. These youngsters were ready to do anything for him, and they called him their father. There were no barriers. I started liking it. At that time, I heard of an accident involving Mohanji's young daughter. She suffered an 18-foot fall and had head injuries and hemorrhage. It was very serious. His wife also was injured in her head. Suddenly, a gloom spread over the whole group, and there was a rumour that the concert would be called off. I thought, "How can that be? If Mohanji is living his teachings, he will not permit anything to stop. How can a personal matter affect a mission matter?" I felt inclined to visit the hospital. Again, my skeptical mind was in action more than any sympathy. I deeply apologize to Mohanji for any mistake I committed in my mind in this regard. I know Mohanji never judges any person and loves unconditionally. So, I have no guilt in me.

When I reached the hospital, I must admit I was quite surprised. The first thing I saw was an unconscious Mila (Mohanji's daughter) and Mohanji sitting next to her bed, his hand on her head, in deep meditation or communion. There was deep peace on his face. A few people were around the bed. Mohanji sat there for a few minutes and got up as Mila was taken away for examinations. Mohanji was behaving with everyone as if he would otherwise. No anger, no anxiety, no fear and no emotions. He even had a smile on his face. His face calmed everyone. As I was leaving, I heard one person talking about the concert on the phone, perhaps to a concerned volunteer. "The concert must happen. Mohanji said, "The show must go on". Well. My question was answered. The mission is beyond the man.

I visited the hospital twice. Both times, Mohanji's face was calm and free from worries. I watched him from a distance. I could never imagine myself being like this if something should ever happen to my children or my wife. Mohanji's wife Biba was also injured and was in the ICU of the hospital along with Mila. It was indeed an uncomfortable situation. Many people visited the hospital, and many people called Mohanji, offering money and support. He was thanking everyone and refusing offers of all kinds of support. I also heard some people complaining that they were not informed about the accident. I felt amused by this comment. If this happened to any of their family members, would they sit down and start calling people, or would they sit in prayers of healing?

I was totally convinced. Mohanji lives his teachings; his outward expressions reflected his inner peace. If it was not so, panic would have reflected on his face. His little daughter in ICU and he was absolutely calm! A clear sign of walking the talk. It is easy to preach theories. Most *gurus* of today are unmarried. They have no children. They have no domestic responsibilities. Here is one guru who is terrestrially just like us, but, clearly above us in consciousness. I felt totally blessed. This incident and my visit to the hospital changed me so much, much more than any speeches, meditations or books. I had to see the practical side of a true *guru*. I had to see the truth. Here was the truth.

I must add that Mohanji's followers who were gathered at the hospital also displayed absolute calm and purpose. There was no panic. There was total dedication. More than dedication, there was genuine love and care in their eyes. No wonder Mohanji calls his people, family. The family-ship was visible. Also, there was no over-emphasis of the situation nor any attempt to take undue advantage of anything. The hotel employees of Oberoi where the accident happened told me that, Mohanji and the whole group were perfectly elegant. They had offered rooms to stay in, and many other services but, nobody used anything. A true guru never wants anything, nor will he take advantage of any situation in a selfish way.

I think I have written too much. My name or identity does not matter. Mohanji says that we must be fearless and egoless when we deliver the truth. The truth will protect us. Though I understand this, I come from a very orthodox, skeptical family and so would like to keep my identity confidential. However, I want the world to know about Mohanji, the way I have seen him. He is a true master who walks his talk. The biggest test would have been concerning his own child, especially since he has gone through many personal pains in his past. He remained totally calm and elegant even during a deep crisis of this kind. I would compare it in terms of my own state if it were me in that situation. A crisis tells the truth. What brings forth this equanimity? Total faith. Total conviction in the tradition and God. Total faith in oneself. This one lives his teachings. Mastering crises. He walks his talk 100%.

I sincerely apologize to any of Mohanji's followers who may be hurt by my bold statements. I was inspired to write by all those who are bravely sharing their own experiences through Mohanji's blogs. More than anything, I am writing this for myself. Mohanji does not need our certificate or appreciation. But, we need these sharings to further our own conviction. The world also needs our testimonials. Many are searching for the right guide, and the right path and our words and testimonials may help someone. We are all pieces of the puzzle; every fragment has importance and relevance.

"Wake up and remember me with love, I shall be with you the whole day. Go to sleep, remembering me with love; I shall be with you through the night."

Mohanji

Mohanji & Nikita Naredi

MASTER'S GRACE IN KAILASH

Nikita Naredi, India

August 2020

Journey to the mighty Kailash happens only through grace and eligibility. Nikita shares her deep insights on how the process was set in motion; she was actually 'called' to Kailash. During this trip, she assisted many people as a doctor and went through the transformation that this abode of Shiva bestows on a true seeker.

Travelling to Kailash was never in my bucket list until a few years back. I had heard many devotees' experiences and had even read the book, 'Kailash with Mohanji' in bits and parts. It was mesmerising to read and hear about Kailash and the *'Kailashis'*, but nothing stirred me enough to consider my trip to Kailash; probably Shiva did not consider me eligible at that time. Kirti Khandelwal, a beautiful member of Mohanji Family from Pune, would always nudge me, "*Didi*, you must go to Kailash," and I would brush it aside thinking I am not physically or psychologically fit enough.

It was again in 2018; I had to go on an official trip to Rajasthan for a fortnight when Kirti reminded me about considering my journey to Kailash.

She also asked me to read the book 'Inner Kora' which is a compilation of the experiences written by the devotees who were fortunate enough to circumambulate the inner Kora of Kailash along with Mohanji. She thought reading the book would inspire me to consider the Kailash *yatra* as it had done to so many others.

I had this book with me since the 2017 Rishikesh retreat where Mohanji himself had blessed and given me this book, but I could somehow never even open the book till then. So, the book accompanied me during this Rajasthan tour of duty. Once I started reading the book, I found it fascinating, and in no time I was devouring page after page. As I neared the end of the book, the yearning to be there in Kailash was taking shape inside me. By the time I finished the other *'Kailashis'* testimonials, this yearning had turned into a resolution. My mind was all ready to be a part of this 'Journey of a lifetime: Kailash with Mohanji.' I believe that this was my 'inner calling.'

Once I decided, the process was set into motion. Kailash is in China; I, being in the Indian Armed Forces, had to seek official permission to travel abroad. Before this permission, the permission of our very own 'Shiva' had to be taken to confirm my eligibility to step on the holy land of Kailash. The permission came in the form of a reply to my text message to Mohanji – "Go ahead". The grace flowed. The official permission was a cakewalk.

Much later, I was made aware of one of my seniors who had also applied for a trek to Kailash, with some other group, which was rejected. The grace really flowed for me.

With the actual dates of travel creeping in fast, came the excitement and also doubts. Excitement is self-explanatory, but doubt started filling me and consuming me. I was afraid. "Will I be able to manage the trip?" This was bolstered by the fact that I never considered myself to be physically fit and enduring. I could barely jog for a short distance before slowing down to a walk. But the resolution to give it my best shot prompted me to build up my stamina. I started my endurance building with long walks and jogs. But these runs were irregular both due to commitment at work and, at times, procrastination. The only regular thing I was doing in that period was 'surrendering'. I would surrender to my Master, Mohanji, and to the Master of the Universe – Shiva. I would say, "If you have called me, I am sure it is only you who can make me sail through". My husband and my daughter were also very supportive and encouraging throughout the preparation process, and their role in my determination cannot be belittled.

Time flashed by, and we were in Kathmandu on 5th August 2019 to commence our *yatra*. It all started with a beautiful evening '*satsang*' with Mohanji and meeting the other enthusiasts from all over the world; a greater part of them not known but were soon going to become like family.

Being a doctor, my duty for the trip was assigned, and I was briefed by Dhritiman Biswas, whom we fondly know as DB, about my role as a doctor to the group. He also made a statement that day, "Your hands are going to be really full as we proceed". I really didn't understand the weight that the casual statement carried till I finished my Kailash *Parikrama*.

The ensuing day at Kathmandu visiting temples and bonding with the other co-travellers was indeed joyful. The helicopter ride to cross the border was mesmerising, but the long road journeys on the bus and staying at different destinations every other night was getting all of us out of our comfort zones.

We reached Keyrung through an exciting helicopter ride, and the Indian pilgrims were fortunate to reach a day earlier as the crossing-over formalities were smoother. We rested and relaxed before our international counterparts joined us the next day. This stay's highlight was the impromptu *satsang* with Mohanji which commenced at 9:30 pm and culminated at 00:30! What a beautiful session we had; questions answered and blessings showered.

The arduous journey was yet to begin. As we ascended in altitude and the long drives on the bus started, many of us started getting sick—motion sickness, headaches, and nausea: a few ailments common to all. I was not immune to any of these (doctors get ill too), but an invisible grace and energy kept me going and encouraged me to help people with small and big ailments. The altitude was already taking a toll on all of us, and this was evident at Saga.

Along with Riana, a beautiful soul from South Africa who had participated twice before in this sacred journey; I took a round of all the rooms checking on everyone. Some were down with headaches, some with breathlessness and others anorexic. The whole group was spread all over the hotel on different floors. We both were going from one room to another without any difficulty. The 'voltage' for this was being provided by the source. My responsibility as a medical care-giver to the Kailash family was very different from the speciality I practice, but what I was doing at that moment felt new but strangely familiar. A feeling of satisfaction and accomplishment had already settled in, not knowing what lay ahead.

Another arduous journey with both morale and health going up and down, we reached the banks of Manasarovar: Our first destination. Despite the happiness and satisfaction of landing on the holy land; most of the group members were not well that night. Mohanji called me; instructed to take a round of all the rooms and meet all the members of our family and look into their health. Most of them were under the effects of high altitude and the resultant hypoxia. The oxygen levels of a few were down, and we administered oxygen to them. The altitude was already taking a toll on a few.

The next morning everyone was very excited about the dip in the holy lake: a dream of every Hindu. However, due to the new policy by the Chinese government, we were prohibited from doing so. We were sad, but acceptance is what we have been imbibing since we joined the Mohanji family. We were all given our share of water to bathe, and we loved every moment of it when all the members were helping each other with the ice-cold serene divine water chanting 'Om Namah Shivaya.'

Despite the ups and downs, each of us was full of gratitude to the divine, and our Master for getting us to this holy soil, being with us physically and spiritually too. I was beckoned every now and then by my comrades due to their ill-health and never once did I get overwhelmed, moving from one place to the other. The purpose of writing this and reiterating the same facts is to highlight that my journey to Kailash was for this larger purpose. Gratitude to my Master, my *Guru*. My first-aid kit which I was carrying with me was made full use of, and I was thanking my husband, who is also a doctor for cajoling me to carry more of the medicines. Again, I don't take any credit for this because I knew I was being facilitated and empowered by Mohanji to do this job. Had I ever imagined that my profession would be made use of at 18000 feet? Gratitude again to Shiva.

The next morning at Manasarovar, I felt really sick, feverish, with a splitting headache and hardly any energy. As I got out of my room after freshening up, Rajesh Kamath told me, "Big Boss is calling you." He meant Mohanji. His tone was not too assuring. I started wondering if I had faltered anywhere. Let me be frank; feeling a bit apprehensive, I went to Mohanji's room. He looked at me and said, "**Colonel, I want to say something to you. Listen very carefully. You will be compassionate towards everyone when it comes to helping and treating people, but you will not be sympathetic. Do what is correct, and I am with you. Don't listen to anyone when it comes to professional advice.**" He was very stern when he said this. I did not understand an iota of the connotation of his words and just nodded in affirmation. He said again, "Do you understand?" I just said, "Yes." I also told him that I was not feeling too great that morning. He said, "I know it." He asked Ivana, a beautiful Mohanji Transformation Method practitioner, and an accomplished person, in an assertive tone to do a session for me and build a *'Kavacham'* (an armour) around me so that no negativities or physical strain affects me. Believe me, that *Kavacham* was indeed an armour which made me last the entire *Parikrama*.

After Manasarovar, we were to embark on our most solicited journey: the trek around Mount Kailash.

All excited, the whole group assembled at the 'Yam Dwar', which marks the starting point for the circumambulation. It is said that at this sacred site, we have to leave our past behind. As we cross it, we begin a new life all over again. Some on ponies and some on foot like a bunch of small kids embarked on the first day of the *Parikrama*. Everyone was assigned a pony and a porter to assist in the trek.

From now on, everyone had to be on their own, walking at their own pace; walking, soaking in Kailash, chanting mantras, or just being with themselves. The terrain was difficult, but the view and the serenity were breath-taking. The other beautiful aspect was the bonding with the porter and the pony man. After a couple of breaks, the 12 km trek culminated in Dirapuk where we visualised what we were striving for: the North Face of Kailash. It seemed we were in the lap of Shiva's Abode. Every one of us was beaming and gleaming with delight, happiness, and gratitude. It seemed we were so close to the holy mountain. After we had parked ourselves and our luggage in the assigned rooms, a few of us got out to climb a small uphill area to have a closer view of Kailash. Some were clicking pictures, and others sat chanting and meditating. Along with my sister Nikunj who was also there for the Kailash *yatra*, after a few pictures to commemorate our victory of the first lap, we sat down to meditate and listened to 'Shiv Kavacham'. It was indeed an out of the world experience.

Suddenly, I heard someone calling out for me fervently. Someone from our group was really sick, and I was asked to go and attend to her. I rushed down the hill to reach her room. She was lying on the bed, looking very pale and even cyanosed (bluish discolouration). Her heart was beating very fast, and the oxygen levels were very low. After examining her, I was very sure she had suffered an acute insult due to hypoxia. She needed urgent medical care. We were not completely equipped to provide any emergency care except oxygen which I immediately started. Sumeet immediately suggested that another group from a different organisation had a medical camp and that they would be better equipped. Their location was slightly far and that we had to go downhill and again climb up. He asked me, "Doc, will you be able to manage that?" as I had to go and give the medical jargon to retrieve the equipment and drugs. I immediately said, "Yes". We had to go downhill and once I had acquired the things climbing up would have been a challenge, especially in that emergency, when the time was of paramount importance. Even today as I write, I don't know from where I got the energy, strength, stamina, and endurance to keep pace with Sumeet and climb up to reach our halt camp. I gave her the emergency drugs, settled her, but she needed immediate evacuation.

That is when I had to be firm and assertive. I declared she needs to go down to be taken to a hospital right now. I had to face a lot of resistance.

There were many opinions: many felt she would settle down; healing would help her, she had completed the first day of *Parikrama*, and her journey would be incomplete, and so on. But her physical condition was not good. There were senior members in our group with mixed responses, but our dear Mamu said we have to do what the doctor says. Everyone was finally convinced, parallelly, arrangements were made for her transportation. It was getting darker. With assistance, we shifted her to the vehicle; she was taken to Darchen and admitted to the hospital. In medical jargon, she progressed from acute mountain sickness to high altitude pulmonary oedema, which can be fatal if not timely intervened. She was admitted to the hospital for three days, and with medical help and above all Shiva's grace, she was discharged. That is the time when Mohanji's words dawned on me, "**Be compassionate but not sympathetic. Execute what is correct**." It was not me. It was him who was making me take decisions.

The second day of the *Parikrama* is supposed to be the toughest. It entails a very steep climb, much rarer oxygen, and greater altitude when crossing the Dolma La Pass. Enveloped in the divine energy, with blessings from the supreme Parabrahma, we reached Dolma La Pass. It was enthralling; it was unbelievable. Only one trick did the magic, 'Om Namah Shivaya'.

Then came a new dilemma! We could see the beautiful emerald green Gauri Kund; the divine water where *'Maa'* the *Shakti* used to purify herself. Going to Gaurikund is again a daunting task. We all started contemplating whether we could manage or not. I started remembering Deviji's experience of her climb and descent to Gaurikund. During her presentation, she had categorically mentioned the climb up after Gaurikund darshan was the most challenging. I doubted myself again. Would I be able to make it? My porter and the pony man both dissuaded me, but again some inner voice shouted, "You have reached here. Why will you not go to Gaurikund and have a feel of the nectar?" With the other companions, we reached down and were at the banks of Gaurikund. With the mesmerising view of the green water, divinity at its best, we all washed with the holy water and carried some in bottles for our group members who could not make it and our families back home.

As I was ascending, the thoughts kept pouring. What had I done to get this reward? Blessings from my ancestors, my family, my patients, and above all, our living Shiva, our *Guru*. Back at the base camp in the evening after the toughest day, we all felt victorious because what lay ahead for the next day was a cakewalk; the last day of *Parikrama* – the easiest part. We completed our last leg enjoying ourselves, smiling, soaking in the place, collecting memoirs, and finally reached Darchen. Once we were in the hotel, everyone was thanking, appreciating, and encouraging me for the medical help which I could provide by his grace, and it only filled me with gratitude. Meeting our friend who had fallen critically ill was most satisfying.

At that moment, I earnestly wanted to meet Mohanji who was waiting behind at the hotel facilitating our *yatra*, giving all his energy to every member connected to him. We were told he had not consumed any food until the time we were back. He is our Father, Mother, Friend, and Divinity in a living form. I asked Madhu if I could meet him. He fulfils all our desires. I was called. As I reached his room, he was sitting on a chair. I fell at his feet. Tears started rolling down. His words were, "Doctor, you have done an amazing job." His words stirred the level of satisfaction and victory, which probably was even more than the feelings I got from accomplishing the highest degree of my profession. I reaffirmed, "I did not understand the words you had spoken at Manasarovar till I was cornered to take the major decision." He knows everything which is going to unfold; every word he utters has immense connotations.

I bow at his feet for taking me to Kailash; a journey of a lifetime and to do service in this Holy Land!

Here is an offering of faith to this great Master, my beloved Mohanji!

Verses of Faith

'Grace' was just another word
Till You came into our lives
Be it personal, professional or spiritual
Every aspect could feel its vibes

'Gratitude' was just a thank you word
Till You taught us what it means
For life, for breath, for food, for family
To express every moment; has got into our genes

'Surrender' we never comprehended this word
Till we did this to you and saw the change
The persona transformed
So did every speck within our range

'Purity' could be such a meaningful word
Did not we ever realise
It should be in thoughts, words and actions
Your teachings made us to imbibe and prioritise

'God' we knew the word
'Guru' we comprehended the word
But little did we fathom their vastness
Till your presence guided us to light from darkness

July 5 2020

Mohanji & Rekha Murali

THE ART OF FORGIVING

Rekha Murali, India

November 2020

Forgiveness doesn't happen easily. Rekha shares how she used the beautiful tool of the 'Forgiveness Process' created by her loving Master to let go off all the hurts and forgive everyone. Her most important learning from this process was the ability to forgive herself and soar high in freedom.

Since childhood, I have often heard these phrases, "To err is human, to forgive divine" and yet another one, "Forgive and forget". Pondering on these two statements, I felt that I could forgive but never forget. It seemed simple. The minute an incident of the past came to my mind, the person who did it to me appeared in my inner eye along with the situation. So, I felt I could never forget.

Recently, a few incidents hurt and saddened me, causing immense stress, disappointments, upheaval, sadness, anger, etc. You name the emotion, and I felt all that. I felt it was the end. It felt as though things would never lookup. I would die a lonely, sad soul. All that changed through something that Mohanji did and as usual, 'He walked with me!'

I heard about the Forgiveness Process that my *Guru* Mohanji had given to the world. Even then, my first thought I jokingly shared with someone was that I am prepared to do anything as an Acharya, but I am not ready to forgive. The pain and wounds were fresh, and I felt it was not easy. It was indeed my mind fooling me.

As an Acharya, what I had learnt and knew deep within was that I had to forgive and move on. Mohanji always said, **"Forgiveness leads to freedom."**

Slowly with all my other practices, I realised forgiveness, letting go and moving on towards my purpose was the top priority. Soon, I got a wonderful opportunity to practise the Forgiveness Process recorded in Mohanji's voice. Now, this piqued my interest. Whatever Mohanji did was always for my highest good. I was eager to unhook and forgive each and everything. My heart soon craved for the freedom that Mohanji always spoke about.

Finally, I got to do the process as it was offered to all the *Acharyas* for a week. I did not want to miss the opportunity, so I did it all the seven days, although it is not necessary. Needless to say, I was left speechless and awed.

The first time, it was as though I was in the world of Harry Potter, with Mohanji using a magic wand to remove all the deeply embedded memories from within me and dissolve them. What was surprising was that during the process, neither did I remember the people nor the situations. All that I remembered was that I had gone through varied emotions such as anger, hatred, jealousy, guilt, regrets and so on. I felt unappreciated and betrayed. Being a perfectionist, whatever I did was never good enough. So, a sense of unworthiness too seemed to linger.

As Mohanji guided me lovingly through the process in a soothing voice, I was able to unburden myself and soar high for a few minutes with him. I understood with clarity the purpose I was born for, and I visualised my Master holding my hand and guiding me forward, leaving all the unwanted impressions, patterns, and karma behind. As we soared higher and higher, he gently sent me ahead and stayed behind to guide other souls lovingly. This really showed the liberated existence of a Master.

This happened on most of the days that I did the process. The whole process would start with bouts of crying, and my heart would feel so heavy each time, I felt it would burst. I have never ever cried like this before. Soon it would cease, and a feeling of lightness would cover me. I would then follow Mohanji faithfully on my journey.

This entire process of forgiveness showed me my purpose. I realised my purpose is to serve the world with unconditional love, kindness and compassion.

This made me so free and accepting of my situation in life.

Later, thinking about the process, I realised that this Forgiveness Process was not an ordinary, guided process. With each word, the Master was working on me. He was operating from a different frequency, and all that I was expected to do was follow the instructions. As usual, he did his job. He cleared layers of muck that I'd collected over lifetimes. Another strange thing was that although I got to do the process, even if I were delayed and didn't do it at the same time every day, I'd start feeling the emotions exactly at that time.

I was under the impression that it would be easy and with a session or two, I'd be fine. But I can tell you that this process is such a precious gift; it continues to keep you in awareness and helps you to let go of the situations you may encounter in your day-to-day life. It is life-transforming, indeed!

Not only that, I suddenly realised that what I was holding on to, playing the victim and thinking I could never forgive disappeared. I was able to accept the situations and move on. How did that happen? As layers of impressions were getting cleared, I was able to accept myself unconditionally with my weaknesses and strengths and totally forgive myself. Once I accepted myself, forgave myself, it was automatically reflected on the outside; forgiving others, the situations, and the surroundings became easy.

The pain, the scars of the situation and the people who caused it did not matter because, with Mohanji's guidance, I chose freedom, I chose acceptance of myself, I chose to love myself, and I chose the path of liberation.

Here is a poem which I was inspired to write thinking about the transformations after meeting Mohanji. With deep gratitude, I offer this poem to my *Guru* Mohanji.

I AM YOU

My first glance of this man in white
As I opened my eyes from my inner stillness
Gentle and elegant, with a calm poise
He acknowledged all with a beautiful smile.

Here was a man, humble and unassuming
An instant liking, a feeling of comfort
His presence warmed my heart
I realised, I had a friend for life.

The conversations began, of things mundane
To deep sharing of things that bothered
The respect grew and basking in the love
I knew this connection was beyond time.

Guru Leela - Mohanji and I

With time, I knew there was more
To this friend behind the loving smile
The banter turned to devotion
He was my guiding light, my eternal master.

He mirrored my thoughts, he mirrors my actions
He remained poised, he remained still
Unaffected by the tantrums I threw
Giving his all, with kindness and with love.

Oh! How privileged am I?
With faith and trust, I surrender to him
A living master who does his job
With no expectation and with love for all!

Am I really worthy of this love?
The benefits are countless
What can I do but bow my head
With gratitude, love and deep surrender.

The connection deepened and I saw
In the deep recesses of my heart
Shining bright, inside and outside
the recognition; I am you and You are I!

> "Trying to be one with God or Guru is a nice desire. Keep that desire. Because your highest growth happens in your strongest integration."
>
> Mohanji

Painting by Suman Gupta

A LIFE OF PURPOSE

Restituto Oqeundo, Philippines
Translated by Inigo Jesus Conlu

April 2020

Mohanji always speaks about living a life of purpose, and he leaves no stone unturned to help his followers with this. This was how Mohanji reached out to Resty through a volunteer. Through miraculous ways, Resty was able to come out from a life in prison and lead a satisfying life by serving the world.

When I was sentenced and sent to prison, I was terrified. In my first week there, I had to sleep on the floor. What made it worse was being next to a stinking bathroom where I could not sleep because everyone was passing by to get to the toilet. The only time I could rest, and sleep was when all the inmates were already asleep. I can never forget that a cockroach bit me during my first few days, and I really suffered a lot. There was no one that I could ask for help. I got sick because of the heat and congestion, but nobody ever helped me. No one would take care of me inside the prison cell. I also suffered from separation anxiety, missing my wife and my son BJ. There was a group who used to visit us and sing prayers. When this group came and prayed, I could not control my tears as I felt remorse.

When my son BJ visited, he told me that his best friend's (Inigo) mother visits this prison monthly to feed the inmates and conduct *yoga* and meditation. I had no idea to which group she belonged. So every time we had a visitor, I looked forward to meeting her. That's why I pushed myself to attend every programme and participated in it. Then in one visit, I finally recognised someone I knew, and she was Irene. She mentioned that a lady named Wee was looking for me. I later found out that she is the mother of Inigo. I was overwhelmed with shame, knowing that Wee knew what I had done to my family, especially my son BJ. But she never saw me as a bad person, showing only kindness and a desire to really help. During our *yoga* and meditation sessions, my fellow inmates and I had the time to reflect and share happiness. It was as if all our discomforts, sufferings and pains were put aside. We even forgot our problems in those moments. Since then, every last Monday of the month, I would look forward to the meditation group to come and have the session with us, because it was not only me who was excited but also my fellow inmates.

What really made me change was when Wee gave me the responsibility to look after the free library placed inside the prison. This made me realise that people still value me and still show their love and trust. And as the days went by, I started to realise the difficulty of living with my family and peers' absence. But this made me look within, and I found myself learning how to pray and seek a closer relationship with Jesus. There were so many hindrances to all my hearings that I never saw as something negative but used them to build hope and strength.

Then, in one of the group's visits, Wee introduced her meditation teacher to all of us, and she even left his picture with me when they left. Little did I know that the man in the picture would change my life forever! The man in the picture, as said by Wee, was miraculous Mohanji. Wee explained that Mohanji was not a God. She told me that Mohanji was a man who has given himself to help the world, bring out the world's goodness, and create changes through meditation, *yoga*, and selfless service. She said that Mohanji sends love, help, and guidance to those who seek. It made me curious. So I asked Wee more about Mohanji, and she would tell me that whenever I feel down with life, I could talk to Mohanji and ask for guidance because he always listens. Some of my inmates asked me about him, so I just shared with them who Mohanji was, as Wee explained.

From that day on, I placed his picture beside Mama Mary and Jesus and started the practice of praying and silencing the mind. Every night, I would pray to Jesus and talk to Mohanji. I always asked for guidance and forgiveness and a second chance to renew my life. As the days, weeks, and months went by, I was still waiting for the dream of getting out of the prison, and despite the delays, I never lost hope. I also promised Wee that I would join her group to inspire others once I get out. As I practised meditation, it made me calm and relaxed, removing all the discomforts felt inside. Sometimes I would fall asleep but be conscious in my body. I felt happier even in my situation; I also felt acceptance of my time there. I started feeling inner peace even on hot days or lonely nights inside the cell.

It was already a year and a half, and it felt like I had been there forever. Then on one random day, the warden called me and asked me to come to his office. He informed me that my name was on the list of inmates who will have a hearing the next day. I was surprised to know this as I was not expecting this news at that time. On that hearing, I was finally allowed to be released and be under probation for a year, for using drugs. It felt like a miracle, but then I realised that the universe was working for me to have a new life. The chance that Wee's group gave me helped me to learn the values of self-love and self-worth. I realised that if others can see value in me, I could also do it. I now know that life should be lived with a purpose and not just wasting it with things that will be harmful to me and others.

A Life Of Purpose

The day arrived when I was finally going to step out of prison. So many inmates were asking for my clothes and other belongings. I decided to leave everything with them except for my pillow and the picture of Mohanji. As I left the place, I hoped and prayed that my inmates would look at me as a symbol of hope for them. I am a free man now; the world outside welcomed me with a bright sunny day. My son had a big smile on his face as he welcomed me, waiting for me outside. Up to this day, I still talk to Mohanji as if he is there in front of me, always asking his guidance every day, as I continue serving people through the Mohanji Philippines group lead by Wee, of which I am now a part.

Mohanji & Rowena Conlu

LOVE TRANSFORMS

Rowena Conlu, Philippines

May 2020

Rowena had never met Mohanji when she plunged into selfless service in the Philippines. She experienced Mohanji's infinite power and consciousness only through these beautiful acts of love. She reached out to many children and in particular a little girl affected by cerebral palsy. Today, she leads a happy and contented life working for the underprivileged in the society with unconditional love and immense faith in the Guru.

Knowing and meeting these little angels allowed me to witness God's transforming power of love!

Our meditation group found Danica, a 12-year-old girl affected by cerebral palsy and meningitis, living in the coastal area of Cogon. She is the third in a family of eight children. Her father is a fisherman, and her mother died of a heart ailment in 2017. When the group found her, she was skin and bones, dying of malnutrition. Her father, Darry, was in despair because of the death of his wife.

Immediately, the group supported her family with food supplies for three of the younger children.

Danica was on a liquid diet, so we got her a blender. Being a widow myself, I felt in my heart the hardship a single parent goes through, mentally and emotionally. I also connected Danica to a doctor friend who kindly committed to checking up on her every week and supplied her with vitamins. We also supported the father by giving him work in our hotel as a groundsman.

I was new to the Mohanji family when I met Danica, and I was doing some *seva* activities in a few places where possible. In 2019, I also started a kids/teen *yoga* and meditation programme. My dream was to share this consciousness to the kids to have a better life in the future. So being in contact with Danica's family, I asked Darlyn her younger sister, to ask her friends if they would like to learn *yoga*.

This became the first group of Mohanji teens/kids. Danica's siblings and some of her friends joined the *yoga* sessions. At that time, I started practising Mohanji's teachings about non-doership, living a life of surrender to God, selflessness, love, kindness, and compassion. I believe this is the perfect example of the transforming power of love. Danica thrives not only with good nutrition but by the love, support, and hope given to her family. We are all a part of the pure universal energy, and that is what Danica feels when we are around her.

The group of 10 kids I started with has now grown to 35. The numbers increase every week, and we are serving two areas here in Roxas City. Children from the coastal regions and also from the central city join us for our sessions regularly. It gives me a lot of joy to be able to help so many people in my community.

Mohanji teens/kids

'Meditation Garden' is what we call our group. We are a group of meditation students using Mohanji's guided meditations that we found online. It's been almost two years since we started feeding those who needed support and introducing *yoga* and meditation in practically all areas here in our province. Once I asked myself, "How are these activities going to be effective to people if we do not go back and encourage them to do the sessions regularly?"

It was February 2019 when a thought came to mind, 'What if I gather the kids here in my place every week and teach them *yoga* and meditation, and give them vegetarian snacks?'

So I sent Darlyn a message: Danica's sister, the person with a disability our group was looking after, near a coastal area. One Sunday, Darlyn gathered her friends and siblings and attended my first *yoga* and meditation session. We did some light *yoga* stretching, breathing techniques, and a short silence as an introduction and had healthy snacks afterwards. Then, I asked them to write down their experiences in a journal to monitor their progress.

The next week, another five kids from the same area joined us to do the same activities. On the third week, Mataji invited five kids from another underprivileged area in the city, and every week the numbers are increasing. At the start, I thought the children were coming because they like the food since most of them are from low-income families. But there are days when they hardly finish the food. And as I observe them, what I realised was, what they love in our meetings were the hugs, the conversations, and the games we play with them because the parents hardly have time with their kids, they feel unloved.

It's been a year already. Now, these kids have developed mindfulness through *yoga*; their behaviour has changed for the better. Even the ways they dress has changed, they are always clean and smell good, and are ready to learn new things. They have learnt to share with the other kids and take them for our *seva* activities in different communities. We are introducing them slowly to chakras, some of Mohanji's teachings like *ahimsa*, selflessness, etc. They love wearing their Mohanji t-shirts and wish to meet Mohanji in person. I gave each child a framed picture of Mohanji as a gift and shared that they can always talk to him because he is like a Father. He is someone who loves them, cares for them, and only wants the best for them.

Love Transforms

Now, even some of the mothers are joining the kids every Sunday for our sessions.

I am very grateful for the beautiful opportunities to help these children and their families. It's lovely to see how love can transform so many lives.

Mohanji & Shyama Jeyaseelan

FAITH AND FEARLESSNESS

Shyama Jeyaseelan, UK

May 2020

Shyama experienced various forms of devotion in her connection with Mohanji. She soon realised how these beautiful and transformational experiences gave her the inner stability and strength to carry on with her frontline work and serve the society when the whole world was affected by the recent pandemic.

In May 2018, towards the end of the *Kriya* Intensive programme and Volunteers Meet in Bosnia, some of us spoke about our experiences with Mohanji in the main *satsang* hall. We sat in a circle, sharing our heartfelt feelings and emotions, all of us absorbed in Mohanji's love and compassion. When it was my turn, I sang a *bhajan* close to my heart, one that I often sing at home to Mohanji. The words are simple yet so beautiful.

**You are the centre of my life, my Lord;
you are the centre of my day.**

**I open my heart to you and pray for
your grace.**

**I feel the power of your love, my Lord,
I feel the power of your love.**

**I open my heart to you and pray for
your grace.**

As I finished, Deviji, who was also seated with us, said with a lovely smile, "I am looking forward to meeting all the bhakti yogis in London soon." A visit by Mohanji, Deviji, and little Mila was taking place in August 2018, and we were all counting the days for their arrival with much excitement, looking forward to having them with us.

During their stay in London, many of us had the privilege of spending some time with Mohanji, Deviji, and Mila. So many beautiful moments, full of grace and joy, filled our days. Those few days flew by quickly, and it was time to say goodbye too soon. Afterwards, as I read the blogs and testimonials from others, I realised how each of us experienced Mohanji's presence and love in our unique way. We may have all been with him simultaneously during the same programme or event, but each one of us experienced him according to our constitution, perception, and eligibility.

During this visit, every moment I spent with Mohanji gave me a different emotion to the feeling of devotion. I recently read a beautiful article on 'Nava vidha bhakti,' the nine forms of devotion. I realised that I had experienced these beautiful emotions and recognised them as such, purely because of Mohanji's grace.

It is said that of the different types of yoga, bhakti yoga is the easiest way to reach the Lord in the *Kaliyuga*. When devotion and love for the Lord are pure, free from conditions, desires, and ego, transformation happens within us. We become the instrument of the Lord. Through writing this article, I pray that my love for Mohanji becomes deeper and purer. May devotion fill my days and bring positive transformations within me.

The nine forms of devotion which we feel and experience towards our *Guru* or God are *shravanam, kirtanam, smaranam, paada sevanam, archanam, vandanam, daasyam, saakhyam, and aatma nivedanam.*

The first in the nine forms of devotion, **shravanam**, is to listen to the divine glories of our *Guru* or God. As we listen and contemplate on his words, qualities, and divine plays, our mind merges with the thoughts of divinity. With easy access to social media, listening to *satsangs*, bhajans, and songs, seeing messages on WhatsApp or Facebook were all tools for me to hear or read about Mohanji throughout the day. Listening to his teachings, seeing his messages and reading others' experiences were all ways for me to connect to him while being away from his physical presence.

Planning his visit with the UK team was exciting, and that itself was a *satsang* too.

As I constantly listened and contemplated on Mohanji, love, and reverence subconsciously grew, and I realised that these thoughts purified me in tangible and subtle ways. As we cultivate a yearning to listen to his glory and teachings with faith, and as we practise what we have learnt, the act of *shravanam* helps us evolve in the journey of spirituality.

In the second form of devotion, **kirtanam**, one sings *Guru* or God's glory with devotion. Whenever we recite or chant his name and sing his glory from the heart, we automatically become joyous; our hearts are filled with love, not just for our dearest *Guru* but also for all those around us. Continuous chanting has the power to elevate us.

At the UK retreat, we had bhajans at the end of each day. Even if he were tired, Mohanji would stay and listen to everyone's offering of love to him, have a *satsang* with us afterwards, before retiring to his room. One of the highlights was to listen to Mohanji sing 'Garuda Gamana' with one of the devotees. We were mesmerised, listening to his beautiful voice, giving joy not only to the devotee he sang with but to all those assembled there.

One evening, we chanted the Sri Rudram in Mohanji's presence. This chanting is done in praise of Lord

Shiva, and I was reminded of chanting it at the holy banks of Manasarovar and during the *parikrama* of Kailash. Lord Shiva, who was silent and majestic in Kailash, had taken the form of the compassionate and loving Mohanji who was physically in the room with us. Although thousands of miles apart, the innocence, divinity, and purity that I felt was the same on both occasions, and I felt so blessed to have Mohanji there with us while chanting. None of us wanted these evenings to end!

Smaranam is the third form of devotion, where one constantly remembers their *Guru* or God and his divine qualities. It is said that *namasmarana*, the constant chanting, and remembrance of the divine will help us attain liberation. Remembering and chanting the name of our loving *Guru*, remembering his compassionate form, seeing divinity in nature are all ways of remembering Mohanji's presence in my life.

Whether it's chanting the Mohanji Gayatri, Healing Gayatri or singing devotional songs/bhajans, I feel that simply knowing/remembering that he's always with me, keeps me connected to him, making life the joyous journey it is. As faith and devotion increase, surrendering my actions to him becomes second nature, and from small miracles to large, I feel Mohanji's presence throughout the day. As acceptance and patience increase, pain and suffering are greatly reduced, and I am able to face life with equanimity more and more.

In the fourth form of devotion, **paada sevanam**, one worships their *Guru* or God by surrendering all actions at his feet and serving him. Recognising that a true *Guru* is connected to the supreme consciousness, worshipping the *paduka* (sanctified sandals) is also a form of *paada sevanam*.

In the Indian tradition, people often refer to the *Guru* or God's feet as *paada pankajam* (lotus feet), as they are described as soft and beautiful like the petals of a lotus. During this visit, we had the incredible opportunity of doing *pada puja* to Mohanji's feet. It was such a sacred event, and all those who took part felt so blessed. Mohanji explained the significance of this sacred ritual and graciously allowed us to wash, decorate and do *aarati* to his feet. It was a dream come true; something many of us had yearned for but had not expected to happen.

Bowing down at the feet of someone, shows humility and lack of ego. As we bow down at the feet of our dearest *Guru* with an innate sense of surrender, we recognise his divinity and pray that he will grant us protection and lead us from the many bindings of life to freedom in existence.

In the fifth form of devotion, **archanam**, one makes an 'offering' of love to their *Guru* or God. It may be ritualistic worship where food, flowers, and many other materialistic items are offered. It can also be singing bhajans, chanting the *sahasranamam*

(1000 names), *ashtothram* (108 names) or doing *aarati*, which are all forms of *archanam*. When the rituals are combined with internal meditation and awareness, our hearts and minds are purified.

While Mohanji was in London, I had the opportunity to make some of his meals with a few other devotees. Cooking is usually not my passion, but making food for Mohanji is a blessing I will always cherish. I can only imagine this would be how Yashoda felt when she made food for Krishna! Mohanji's enjoyment of simple food is lovely to witness.

The times I spent in the kitchen gave me such a close connection to Mohanji. Nothing else existed apart from him. In those moments, I was not a parent, wife, sister or daughter. There was no personality, just a beautiful feeling of not existing as a person with ego, etc., but being an empty instrument for divinity to work through. This state of perpetual meditation which seemed beyond my reach seems a little closer to attain now, a state I should attempt to be in, throughout the day.

My *archanam* or offering while Mohanji was here in the physical form for a few fleeting days has enabled me to surrender and offer all my actions to him even when he's physically not present. Expressing our love for him and connecting to him with mind and heart, all our activities become sacred when offered at the feet of the *Guru*.

The sixth form of devotion is reverential prayer, **vandanam**, to our *Guru* or God. Prayer is the heart's language, and when expressed with sincerity and love, it becomes an intensely personal process that elevates us. There are many types of prayers; of gratitude, the well-being of others, peace, etc.

Prayers and chanting have become a part of life, and I realise Mohanji purifies us in subtle ways when we undertake these actions with the correct intent. Whether it's chanting, singing or simply talking to Mohanji in my mind and seeing answers to my questions or thoughts through someone or something, my faith in prayers has increased manifold. Whether it's an internal dialogue or an outward expression, prayers make me feel closer to Mohanji. I share an incident here, which showed me again he knows everything that we think, say or do, that we always live in the presence of divinity.

On the last night before Mohanji's family left, I was feeling so sad. I sent a text message to the host family, saying, "Tomorrow morning will be the last meal with Mohanji for a while." I had not asked to help make breakfast as I knew someone else was bringing food in the morning but went to help with other things. Just a short time before leaving for the airport, Mohanji said, "Let's have some *upma*." I thought He was joking as He knew someone was bringing breakfast and said, "Mohanji, are you serious?" He replied with a smile "I never joke about food." As we rushed about in the kitchen with last-minute preparations, I realised that Mohanji knew my thoughts and feelings and in his usual compassionate way, asked me to make something to make me happy. Always so caring and loving, he spreads joy in every possible way. That morning we had two different items for breakfast, blessed by Mohanji!

In the seventh form of devotion, **daasyam**, one aspires to be of personal service to their *Guru* or God. With no sense of inferiority, one yearns to serve the *Guru* as well as his devotees. Only those who are trustworthy, truly humble and are not self-centred are given this boon, and it's amazing to see Mohanji's interaction with such beautiful people. He's so relaxed and happy in the midst of those who love him unconditionally and serve him selflessly.

Hanuman's devotion to Lord Rama is a great example of *daasyam*. I have heard Mohanji speak of Hanuman with so much love and share a story he narrated a couple of years ago. When Valmiki completed the epic Ramayana, Sage Narada who read it said that Hanuman's Ramayana was better. Valmiki was not happy that a 'monkey' had also written a Ramayana and wanted to find out if it was better.

Valmiki found Hanuman in *Kadali-vana* (plantain grove), and the Ramayana inscribed on the broad plantain leaves. Reading it, he found it to be exquisite and unable to help himself, started to cry. When Hanuman asked if it was that bad, Valmiki replied he was crying because it was so beautiful and no one would read his Ramayana once they read Hanuman's Ramayana.

Hearing this Hanuman tore up the banana leaves and said, no one will read Hanuman's Ramayana. You wrote it so that the world remembers you, but I wrote it so that I remember Ram." Hearing this story of Hanuman's pure love for Lord Rama in Mohanji's mesmerising voice was amazing, and it brought tears to my eyes. Even now, when I think back to this moment, I feel so humbled to be a part of Mohanji's family, receiving his love and grace, and pray that such intense devotion and purity wells within me too.

In the eighth form of devotion, **saakhyam**, the devotee considers the *Guru* or God their friend. An example of this is Lord Krishna's childhood in Vrindavan. He spent the days playing with his friends and taking care of the cows. His friends would chase him while playing, massage his legs while resting and feed him food with love. Their love for Krishna was complete. Mohanji is also our true friend, who accepts us as we are, with no judgements or expectations, interacting with us with pure love.

Faith And Fearlessness

It is always a joy to see Mohanji relaxing at times, away from his back to back programmes.

One evening after Mohanji had retired to his room, a couple of us talked about a song that Mohanji likes, and we were listening to it on YouTube. The next morning while having breakfast, he started talking about the song as if he'd been there during our conversation! He then asked us to play that song and sang along with Sonu Nigam (a famous Indian singer), his deep voice perfectly complementing the singer's higher pitch. Very sweetly, Mohanji would explain the song's meaning to me between singing the verses, as I was the only person there who didn't understand the language. It was a privilege to see Mohanji's carefree attitude and joyous singing. How blessed we are to have the eternal friendship of our *Guru*.

In the ninth form of devotion, **aatma nivedanam**, the devotee surrenders entirely to the *Guru* or God's will with no trace of ego. If filled with devotion, the devotee gains knowledge of his true self and becomes one with the divine, and all aspects of his creation. When we offer everything to our *Guru* with equanimity, we become his instruments, and the *Guru* takes complete care. He knows what is right for us; all we need is trust and full faith.

Mohanji is a living example of simplicity and humility. He teaches us by being a true inspiration. Mohanji encourages us to serve with love and humility, not just those who visit him or are in his fold, but all beings of the Earth, to the best of our capacity. By cultivating love and serving the needy, we realise the existence of divinity in all forms.

Taking up one or a number of these paths to connect with our beloved *Guru*, understanding the path and following it with faith and consistency, we can make our lives purposeful and meaningful. We become the pure instruments of the *Guru*, spreading unity, purity, and divinity to the world.

> *"Worshipping the Guru, considering him as representing the Lord Almighty or personification of the Lord is definitely the path of those who are inclined to bhakti or devotional path of spirituality."* – Mohanji

Nearly two years after this memorable time, Mohanji was going to revisit us in March 2020. Amidst much preparation, planning and excitement, we were counting the days for Mohanji to come. Little did any of us know what we would be facing this year, an invisible force that was about to shake the whole world! Just a couple of days before Mohanji's travel, the World Health Organization (WHO) on March 11, 2020, declared the Covid-19 outbreak a global pandemic, and it irrevocably changed our lives!

Although extremely disappointed that we would not see Mohanji as planned, the following months brought about new awareness and positive changes within me, helping me realise more and more that physical proximity to our *Guru* may not always be possible, but he is very much with us in consciousness.

Having experienced many different ways of devotion and connection to Mohanji (remembrance, chanting, singing, prayers, service, friendship, faith and surrender) helped me immensely during the ongoing challenges we were facing daily. This deep connection gave me inner stability and strength, and spontaneous compassion and motivation to help others at this difficult time. I share here an experience I had written during the pandemic.

It is the second week of May. The UK finally sees a decline in the spreading of the Covid-19 virus. Lockdown measures are slightly relaxed, although restrictions for travel, school, shopping, socialising, and the elderly, as many other areas continue. After losing thousands of lives and devastation to so many families, we hope that life will return to relative normalcy soon.

The UK is one of the countries to be severely affected during the pandemic. During the peak time in April, nearly a thousand lives were lost daily. Fighting this invisible force was a huge challenge for the country, as it was for the rest of the world.

During this time, we all faced many other challenges too. Many people lost their livelihood. No jobs meant little or no income to support our families. While many people were asked to work from home, front line workers had to continue to work, potentially risking their lives daily. The National Health Service (NHS) struggled to support its staff with adequate personal protective equipment (PPE). Many NHS staff members fell ill, and sadly many lives were also lost.

Despite all these challenges, the human spirit survived. We saw so many charities and organisations coming forward to support and help the NHS, to help the elderly and the vulnerable, to support those who had lost their jobs. Mohanji ACT Foundation team also came forward to help wherever possible with many acts of kindness.

With generous donations from the Mohanji UK family, food donations were made to local NHS hospitals to help the staff. This meant that many did not need to face a long shopping queue at the end of a long and stressful working day. Food donations were made to food-banks where those without jobs come and receive supplies to help them with their daily essentials.

Faith And Fearlessness

While workplaces brought many changes to most people; my work continued as normal as an NHS worker. It also meant that social distancing was impossible; I had to make physical contact with patients as before. There was no PPE for regular ultrasound scan sessions, only when coming in contact with confirmed Covid-19 patients. During the first few weeks, we did not even have masks to wear.

We have all learnt that life will always bring challenges, some harder than others, but when *Guru's* grace and protection are present, we are immune to daily life shocks. This is something I have seen in so many ways within this short time. During our Acharya training, I remember Mohanji saying many times, **"The Tradition is with you. Be fearless. Be compassionate and loving. Serve society."**

This reassurance and guidance were definitely in need at this time of crisis. With Mohanji's grace, there was no fear of the disease in me, whether at work or during service activities. Any of my patients could be carriers of the virus or be in the incubation period of developing the illness. Never once did Mohanji allow a drop of fear to come in my thoughts. When people ask if it's stressful going to work, the answer was truthful, and cheerful, "No, I'm ok." Fear, worry or anxiety would have reduced my immune system and made me vulnerable to falling ill, and Mohanji made sure I felt stable within.

It was also nice to share that stability and positive attitude with my colleagues; it helped us have a relatively normal work environment.

All the *Acharyas* and other Mohanji Foundation volunteers were doing online programmes inspired by Mohanji. My resistance to learning to use new technology, fear of facing a live camera, and all other feelings of insecurities melted away as we all realised the importance of doing these online activities. Reaching out to as many people as possible with love and bringing positivity when so many people were facing various fears was paramount.

Amongst the various programmes, we were also chanting the Gayatri *mantra* and the Maha Mrithyunjaya *mantra* every day, intending to bring love, light and positive energy to Mother Earth and all her beings. This was benefitting us immensely too. The energy and the vibrations of the chanting were energising and rejuvenating, increasing our immunity. When I received unusually high numbers of requests for distant Mai-Tri sessions, I realised the amount of healing Mohanji gave me. How beautifully he takes care of us, whether we realise it or not.

Many of the ACT volunteers could not physically help with food donations due to various reasons. This meant that I was able to help often, and it was a privilege to have the opportunity to help the

NHS staff, the Covid hub staff and the homeless shelters by distributing essential food supplies. It was a heart-touching moment to see the doctors' happy faces when a volunteer took ice-cream bars to a local accident and emergency department. Mohanji has given us this amazing platform to make a difference in our local communities and positively contribute. It's truly wonderful to be a part of it.

Mohanji has said this period in confinement is a time for contemplation and reflection.

Nature has given us time to slow down and to reassess what is truly important in our lives. It has been a time for me to appreciate my time with the family. With universities and schools closed, my children are home, and it's lovely to be together, tease them, laugh, and enjoy their company. It's great to play with our cats in the garden. We have been blessed with warm weather on most days, and it has given me the time to sit in the garden and enjoy nature, to connect with the elements. This is something I have not done in years.

Social media has brought the global family to our homes. Friends and relatives, whom I have not spoken to or made contact in many months, have been in touch. It has been a time to reconnect and to ensure the well-being of our dear ones. Even my parents who are in their 80s facetime us to see the cats!

I'm truly grateful for the many moments of grace that have been possible only because of Mohanji. Thank you, Mohanji for your presence in our lives, guiding us, and for the platforms to serve the society with love, compassion, and kindness. Thank you for inspiring us with your words and actions to serve selflessly and fearlessly.

> "All you need is the lamp of faith. Life will beautifully reveal itself. Let no winds of life blow out the flame of faith in yourself and in the grace of God."
>
> Mohanji

Mohanji & Subhasree Thottungal

COMPASSION UNLIMITED

Subhasree Thottungal, UK

December 2020

It is said that a Guru is compassion incarnate and fulfils every wish of the follower to make them ready to walk the path of liberation. In this beautiful write-up, Subhasree shares how some of her innermost thoughts and wishes were fulfilled in miraculous ways along with physical healing by Mohanji even though she had not voiced them. The Guru knows everything!

Being with Mohanji, over time, I have realised that we never need to ask anything, we never need to tell him anything. He feels our thoughts, responds appropriately, and he even fulfils our desires too.

In this write-up, I will express a few such experiences, which made me wonder how compassionately Mohanji fulfilled my wishes and how he removed my pain and probably took it on himself! It may sound difficult to believe unless you really see with your own eyes.

In today's logical world, does this really happen? I would probably have not believed if this didn't happen to me directly. One thing for sure, with Mohanji, nothing ever is a coincidence!

So here it goes.

Sometime back in 2018, I think Mohanji had travelled to Mookambika (Kollur in Karnataka), and there were photos of him on FB. When I had seen those photos, I had a thought at that time that may be one day I should go to Mookambika with Mohanji. That desire remained there.

In 2019, around Sep/Oct, a *Kriya* Intensive retreat was announced in Mookambika for December 2019. I was thrilled to hear this and thought that I would go for that. But soon, I realised the dates were such that I wouldn't be able to make it because I was going to the Philippines for an *Acharya* Program for about a week and I would just be returning around this time. The visit to the Philippines was on Mohanji's advise, and so that couldn't be compromised. I had accepted that I wouldn't be able to attend the *Kriya* intensive and miss going to Mookambika with Mohanji.

Anyway, the days went by. I completed my Philippines trip. After that, a few days with my in-laws and parents were over; it was time to return to London at the beginning of Jan 2020. I knew Mohanji was in Bangalore and since my return flight to London was from Bangalore, I thought of checking with Mohanji if I could meet him. I messaged him, and he said I could come and meet him, but he is not in Bangalore. He was in isolation and at Mookambika. But he welcomed me to go and meet him there and asked me to check with Preeti *didi* regarding the travel details. I was speechless! Mohanji had called me to visit him in Mookambika!

I instantly understood and realised that Mohanji was fulfilling my desire of visiting Mookambika with him, which I missed earlier because I had to go to the Philippines! My heart truly expanded with gratitude. Anyway, I travelled as Preeti *didi* kindly made all the necessary arrangements. Those days, I had immense pain in my feet, my Rheumatoid Arthritis pain in my feet had flared up just before the visit to the Philippines. During this whole trip, the pain was intense, and I was limping.

Anyway, I reached Mookambika. Rajesh Kamath and another devotee who was accompanying Mohanji received me. When I met Mohanji, he noticed me limping and asked me about it. I just brushed it aside. I was too happy just seeing Mohanji.

Mohanji said, early next morning, before 5 am, we will be going to the temple and to stand in the queue to have the "Nirmalya Darshan" – the first view of Mother Goddess. Every moment with Mohanji is so special. We were ready by 4:30 am and walked barefooted to the temple and stood outside, waiting for the door to open. Mohanji was behaving just like any other ordinary visitor, waiting at the side, very humbly. A Master of his stature to wait outside the temple patiently gave us the teaching of pure humility, no ego, no demand of comfort!

While I was standing by his side, he suddenly called me and taught me a breathing exercise. While receiving this *Diksha* from my *Guru* standing in front of Mother's temple, I even had no sense to feel good about it - mind, ego and pride had evaporated at that time, and it was only bliss. The bliss of receiving *Guru*'s grace!

Soon the temple door opened and we went inside. I was behind Mohanji. We all stood at the front in the queue; Mohanji asked me to come in front of him and stand. I felt a little awkward to stand in front of Mohanji. But he made sure that I stood right in front to see Mother and the rituals clearly without any obstruction! I had a special prayer to make. (I will write about it on a later date) When the ritual was going on, I made this prayer, being fully aware that my *Guru* is standing behind me with his grace engulfing me totally. Suddenly as I opened my eyes, I saw a flower from Mother's head had dropped. We believe that the flower dropping from the head of the idol is a symbol that God has accepted our prayer!

I immediately turned around, trying to look at Mohanji, and he had a smile on his face! While this early morning ritual was happening, Mohanji was narrating to me all the ritual details. Just like a father or mother would explain to their child for the first time. He ensured that I had a clear view too. After the rituals, Mohanji went to the side of the temple, and there was a special veranda where people usually sit and do prayers. This is where Adi Shankaracharya's temple is also present. Mohanji went and sat directly opposite, facing Adi Shankaracharya's temple. Rajesh went and sat nearby.

I was walking slowly, limping and was about to sit a little far away from Mohanji, not wanting to disturb him, as he had his eyes closed. Mohanji opened his eyes and called me to sit next to him, gesturing with his hands to space on his left side. As I sat next to him, it was as if I had entered into a high energy zone. I thought of doing *Kriya* there. Mohanji then reminded me to do the breathing exercise he had taught me while standing outside, to do it just before I do any sadhana. For me, it was already a big deal that Mohanji opened his eyes, called me to sit and was now giving direction to intensify my sadhana. He was not worried about his sadhana; he was guiding me instead! A true *Guru* he is, truly there every moment to guide us! I did as he guided and then did *Kriya*.

During *Kriya* that time, I had a feeling of floating; my bottom couldn't feel the cool hard stone surface any more. I was truly levitating with the power of that energy sphere that I was inside, being right next to Mohanji. This *Kriya* experience was probably a once in a lifetime experience. (Well every meeting, every moment I am with Mohanji, I take it as once in a lifetime moment!) I am sure my words are nowhere near doing justice to what I had experienced that time. I could not feel my breath, heartbeat, or vibration in the body, simply floating.

When I finished *Kriya*, I opened my eyes, Mohanji was sitting very calmly. I wanted to capture that moment, especially the view that I had in front of my eyes, seeing Adi Shankaracharya at one end of the veranda and Mohanji at this end, both facing each other! I took out my phone quietly and clicked a few pics (though we are not supposed to). Mohanji told me to be careful, as the previous day, the camera of a devotee was taken away.

I was sitting and just noticing other devotees in the temple. Everyone was touching their head to the outside wall of the main temple, writing something with their fingers. I was thinking about what they were doing, and Mohanji said people write their wishes there on the wall at that time. I nodded my head. Then he told me to go there and write and ask Mother to remove the pain from my feet. I was probably a bit hesitant to get up and go, and I feel when I am with Mohanji, why do I need to pray for anything for myself, he knows what is needed.

Then Mohanji insisted again, **"Go and ask Mother to remove your pain and make you fit. You have**

a lot of work to do." These were not mere words; this was a command for me. I got up and limped to that place and did as Mohanji had instructed. And then came back and sat next to Mohanji again. We sat there for a couple of hours almost till the *aarati* happens. While we were sitting, an old lady came. In the last few days of Mohanji's regular visits and sitting at the same place, they had got to know each other, and so she comes and talks to Mohanji in their language – Malayalam.

When she saw me, Mohanji first introduced me to her in their language as his *'shishya'* which means 'disciple'. For me to hear this word directly from Mohanji, it was a great thing inside this pious temple in front of Adi Shankaracharya. I can be his follower, I can be his devotee, but to be my *Guru*'s disciple is a lifetime honour itself! Then he requested the lady to help me go and see the *aarati* properly right in the front again.

Mohanji was not going there, but he ensured that we were taken care of and had a proper *darshan*. Before going out, we did the *parikrama* around the temple visiting all the other small temples of other deities, and Mohanji continued to talk to me about each one. He even instructed Rajesh to get two lamps for me and showed me where to light it, show it, and place those lamps! Honestly, I was a 5-year-old girl at that time, and my father was showing me around everything with so much care and compassion. I was still floating!

I stayed one more day in Mookambika and those two days watching Mohanji being in a sadhana mode; I felt it was my *punya* from many lifetimes! I returned to London to determine that I would meet Mohanji again in a few weeks for the Global Summit and Mohanji's birthday celebration in Sri Lanka.

At the end of January, it was the inauguration of the land in Arunachala – a home for seniors. I heard from some people who met Mohanji at that time that he had terrible pain in his feet and was limping. A few weeks later, during the 3rd week of February, we all travelled to Sri Lanka. When I reached the hotel, and after some time, I got the chance to meet Mohanji in his room. And what I saw made me go numb. His left foot was very swollen, and he was in pain.

It didn't take me a moment to realise what had happened since January first week when I was limping in front of him with swelling and pain in my left foot, and now I was walking fine, but he had swelling and pain in his left foot. I am insignificant here. What is significant is his compassion. He had transferred my pain, making me fit! His words in Mookambika temple were ringing in my ears, **"Tell Mother to make you fit. You have a lot of work to do."**

After the Global Summit, on this birthday morning, we all went to Kataragama temple. While walking around the temple, Mohanji was limping. Even though he had pain, nothing was shown on his face; he laughed and talked with everyone. Inside the temple, on the sandy ground, he was walking barefooted and was limping. At that point, I couldn't stop my emotion anymore. My heart was crying out. When I got the chance, I expressed to him, "Mohanji, please give back my pain to me. I can't see you like this." He smiled and said, **"How do you know it's only yours? You can't bear what I can. I may have some pain in the body, but I have no suffering."**

It was the responsibility of a mother who would bear all the pain for the child but will never make it visible to the child. Mohanji doesn't need any credit for what he does for us. His only aim is to free us from our pain and suffering without making it a big deal in front of us. He does his job quietly. On one side, I was so grateful to him to have removed my pain and made me fit, but I was sad to see him in that pain on another side.

One evening while we were in some discussion during the global meet, Barbara called me to say Mohanji had called me. That evening Mohanji was not feeling well. When I went to his room, he was resting. When I went near him, he opened his palm and showed me a thread that he was holding. It was a part of his *janeyu* (the sacred thread that he wears around his neck and chest). He said while he was laying there his hand on his chest, half of the *janeyu* just came in his hand, he doesn't know-how.

He still has the *janeyu* around his chest. He gave me that sacred thread in my hand and told me to keep it.

It was no less than a miracle, that while he was sleeping, a few layers of the sacred thread came in his hand just like that! I didn't use my mind to analyse this or to understand this. For me, it was my *Guru*'s blessings, his protection, in the form of the sacred thread, protection that had materialised in his hand! Without any delay, he had called me and given it to me, which meant he knew I needed protection at that time. We have no clue what dangers he protects us and saves us from, some we see, some we don't see and some we see but don't realise. His subtle way of working is beyond the understanding of my limited thinking.

The only thing that I know very well is that his compassion and love are beyond any limit, beyond any boundary. Truly for me, Mohanji is compassion incarnate, showering his grace and love unconditionally beyond any form or relation. My heartfelt gratitude, my hug and love from this tiny heart goes to where my *Guru* lives. Not too far away, but right here, at the centre of my heart. I love you, Mohanji. *Koti Pranaams.*

"You are the brightness. You are the light. You are the earth, wind, water and fire. You are the mind. You are the soul. You are yourself. You are myself. You are everything. You are the salvation that you have been looking for. Look no further. You are that. Love."

Mohanji

Painting by Vishal Mothilall

FREEDOM FROM PATTERNS

Trent Leighton, Canada
December 2020

In this beautiful testimonial of transformation, Trent shares with gratitude how he realised that a true Guru's love is pure and unconditional after his initial uncertainties and doubts. With Mohanji's grace and guidance, he undergoes the transformation from illness and self-indulgence to love and selflessness.

I first encountered Mohanji roughly two years ago through a video on the Sai Baba Speaks YouTube channel. Initially, I was struck by the immediacy and power of his divine transmission but also extremely suspicious that he was intent on poaching devotees of Sai like me from our Guru. As I began to dig deeper into the life and teachings of Mohanji, these doubts and misgivings quickly evaporated. First of all, it was clear to me that Mohanji was, in fact, deepening and authenticating my connection to Baba, not competing against him. Secondly, he was providing an open invitation for me to address long-overdue issues in my life through a practical, real-world spiritually, problems and blind-spots that I had been ignoring for decades by hiding behind a false persona of devotion and second-hand Self-Realization.

Having been involved with a number of teachings, traditions and spiritual communities since my teens, I learned early on the art of the spiritual bypass, which is selfishly using the Guru to escape life demands. In a matter of months, Mohanji completely put the brakes on these deeply entrenched patterns by instilling what I can best describe as an unconditional and loving motherly demand to use his grace to address matters in my life head-on, with firm conviction and faith. At the top of this list was my drug and alcohol abuse that has exacted a huge toll in my life for the past 25 years. I had become an expert in manipulating books, meditations and teachers to hide this reality, the fact that Mohanji not only pointed out but did not let me misuse his realization to perpetuate my addiction.

Every time I attempted to convince myself that getting high would accentuate his meditations, Mohanji would slam the door shut, literally and viscerally. I have never experienced anything like it in my life; the absolute full stop that his watchful eye has provided every time an impulse or urge to use drugs arises. This reality culminated with the *Kriya* training in which Mohanji initiated a series of deep considerations in my life that continue to this day. One afternoon shortly after the training a clear and distinct voice spoke the following "Have you ever stopped to consider Trent that going to treatment for your addiction is the most spiritual decision you can make for yourself right now?" My immediate response was no, I had never entertained such a possibility and in fact, had always viewed substance abuse treatment for those with much more serious addictions than my own.

The most amazing blessing and a testimony to Mohanji is that going to treatment actually happened. He provided me with an opportunity to apply spiritual solutions to a very real problem on September 3rd of this year, where I entered an intensive program for 48 days that has absolutely transformed my life. In the process of confronting years of pain, mental illness, denial and self-indulgence, I learned that 'sobriety' is much more than not using drugs but rather, is about actively embodying the love and selflessness the Master freely provides on a moment to moment basis, regardless of what life presents.

The gratitude and joy I feel from Mohanji are impossible to put into words. He has unequivocally fulfilled his promise to watch over his devotee's every need while blessing me with the realization that the relationship with an authentic Master is reciprocal in nature requiring me to not only receive but to live the teachings by continually giving back.

Mohanji & Vasantha Bhavraju

A DEVOTEE SPEAKS

Vasantha Bhavraju (Tayiji), India
December 2020

Eighty years young, Mrs Vasantha Bhavraju, very lovingly called 'Tayiji' by Mohanji and the entire Mohanji family, shares her experiences of the various dimensions of Mohanji that she sees. For someone with an intense religious background, for whom the Hindu Gods are not mere names or idols, to realise the Guru Principle and see God in Guru comes from a deep understanding. The following write up is from a video testimonial given by Tayiji on her 78th birthday in December 2018.

My first Meeting with Mohanji

Phanidhar, my nephew is a follower of Mohanji. In 2011, Mohanji stepped into our home, where Phanidhar's mother, Shubha and I live. I was shocked to see a different form of a *Guru* than what I had in my mind. Mohanji was very casual, wearing jeans, shoes and his hair was long. My mind had an instant doubt; can a *Guru* be like this? Anyway, we welcomed him with respect; he came inside and sat on the couch. Looking at me, he said, **"Some people are suspicious of me and wonder how someone** wearing denim and shoes can be a *Guru*!" I was taken aback to realise that Mohanji had read my thoughts and I was embarrassed about it.

During our conversation, he casually asked, **"Why did you stop performing the *aarati* for Shirdi Sai Baba?"** Once again I was taken aback, as a past memory popped up. When I used to live in Vijayawada in Andhra Pradesh (India), we used to perform Baba's *aarati* every Thursday, singing all the songs of the *aarati*, exactly how it happens in Shirdi. But somehow I had discontinued this practice after coming to Delhi. I couldn't stop wondering how Mohanji came to know about this and reminded us. He advised us to start Baba's *aarati* again.

Divine experiences with Mohanji - 2012 to 2018:

2012: In the month of May, Mohanji was going to visit Madhuban, a restaurant owned by Sumit, another close devotee of Mohanji and a friend of Phanidhar, in Gurgaon, India. Shubha (known fondly as *Amma*) and I wanted to go and meet him. Mohanji was supposed to arrive there at 5 pm. But just a couple of hours before that, there was such a loud storm between 2-3 pm that the doors started knocking. There was so much rain and dust that we gave up hope of going to Madhuban. Around 3:00 – 3:30 pm, the storm and rain gradually subsided and everything was clean. The sun came out, and we went to Madhuban in the evening to meet

Mohanji. We were surprised that a storm would come suddenly and stop. Sumit was there and said that Mohanji had done a *Yagna* of *Panch Tattva* in a temple in Gurgaon. The storm was a result of that. We were stunned to know that Mohanji's grace was again at play.

Later that year, Mohanji came home on the occasion of *Dussehra*. I requested him to allow me to do his *Pada Puja* (worshipping the feet). Mohanji said, **"You are already doing *Pada Puja* every day, why do it especially now?"** I had been doing *Pada Puja* for Shirdi Baba with devotion every day. I felt that Mohanji receives the *Pada Puja* of Sai Baba that I do. It is the glory of Mohanji which made me realise that all Masters are one.

2013: One day, my son informed me that Mohanji and a group of 10-15 people were coming home for lunch. Shubha, my sister-in-law, wasn't at home those days. I got worried about cooking for so many people, though my daughter-in-law was there to help. Anyway, I woke up early that day, took my bath and lit a lamp in front of Baba and prayed, "*Babaji* is coming to our house with others. Please give me the strength to cook delicious food for everyone." Soon my daughter-in-law and I got busy cooking and preparing different delicacies. When the guests arrived, some of the devotees also helped us in making *rotis* and *papad*. The entire lunch preparation for so many people went so smoothly.

When sitting to eat, Mohanji said to the others, **"She has been up since morning and praying to Baba that she can make delicious food. See how tasty the food is. Have you all eaten?"** The food cooked for 15 people was eaten by more than 25 people. People kept coming and eating that day. This is also one of his great *leelas*.

2015: In the month of June, Mohanji was visiting the *samadhi* of a *Guruji* in Chhatarpur, Delhi. Shubha, a devotee from the UK and I were accompanying Mohanji. Since it was a Thursday, the crowd was quite large and our car was stopped far away. So we had to walk towards *Guruji's samadhi*. I was worrying about walking that far. Mohanji had already gone ahead and was walking very fast. Suddenly he slowed down and he started moving with heavy steps. This reminded me of Mahadev, a TV show. In it, Shiva carries his consort Sati Devi on his shoulders. Finally, we all met near the stand and I shared my observation with Mohanji. He said, **"This was no illusion. I carried both of you on my shoulders because you were saying you can't walk, right? That's why I did it."**

There were many people in the queue that day. Suddenly I had the vision of Shirdi Sai Baba and Sathya Sai Baba. Both were running towards me laughing, raising their hands and blessing me. This vision stayed for some time. I mentioned this vision to Mohanji. He said, **"You were saying in the morning that you do not see any Gods. You were**

feeling sad. That is why I got you their *darshan*. Anyway, all *Gurus* are one." I was speechless! I don't know what sadhana I have done to receive such grace from Mohanji. My joy knew no bounds.

Let me share one more experience. I always used to perform Mohanji's *aarati* in the evening. But I had a habit of watching a TV serial at 6:00 pm. So some days, I would do *aarati* early, or after the serial or during the ad breaks.

After a few days, Mohanji came to our home and he said in front of everyone, "**What is the matter? I come every day and listen to your *aarati*. One day you hurry, one day at 6:00, one day at 6:15. Why are you giving *aarati* like this?**"

He knows everything, but he said this to get rid of that habit of mine. I apologized to him. After that day, I stopped watching the serial and started performing *aarati* at the same time every day.

2016: In April 2016 on the night of the *Purnima* (full moon), I could not sleep. At 2-3 am, I heard my own voice screaming loudly. "Who are you? You have come in a disguise. You are not Mohanji." Then suddenly I heard myself saying, "You are that original element."

In the same month, once I was listening to a *Qawwali* (devotional music of the Sufi sect) on TV. The devotion expressed in the *Qawwali* brought tears to my eyes. Suddenly I had a vision - Mohanji was sitting in a meditation pose at some distance, wearing white clothes. As soon as I saw Mohanji, I started calling him and moving towards him. After taking a few steps, my feet suddenly stopped. I tried to take further steps, but could not lift my feet.

After a few days, Mohanji came home. I asked him about these two experiences. He asked, **"You are writing about my *Charitra*, is it not? I am the core element, now you know it, so write. No one can come to me in their body; they can come only in their consciousness."**

Later, on the day of *Kartik Purnima* that same year, Rajesh Kamath was in our home. Shubha, Rajesh and I performed the rituals of worshipping Lord Shiva. We also accomplished the custom of lighting 364 wicks on *Kartik Purnima*. Mohanji was at home too. When we invited him to join us, he said, **"You continue the ritual. I shall come automatically while lighting the lamp."**

Saying this, he went into the room and closed the door. After lighting the lamp, we offered *prasad* to God and performed *aarati* to Mohanji and Lord Shiva. Then Rajesh and Shubha bowed down to Mohanji and touched his feet. When I went to touch his feet, I noticed a lot of sand on Mohanji's feet. I kept quiet that time but asked him later about it. He replied, **"Today is *Kartik Purnima*, is it not? So**

I went to visit all. That is why there was sand. This is why I wear my dhoti lower, so that no one sees my feet."

2017: I had a fall in March 2017. I had to go through a surgery for hip joint replacement. When I came home after the surgery, Mohanji came to see me. After seeing me, he told my daughter and son, **"A big accident was going to happen. I got her out with an injury on one leg."**

The same day, when I came to know that he was coming, I was welcoming him in spirit in the early morning, by laying roses in the corridor. I saw that instead of Mohanji, Dattatreya came running. There was so much brightness behind him. He was only wearing a dhoti and a *Rudraksha* garland around his neck. There were three heads and only two hands. With rosary beads in one hand and a water pot in another, he was laughing and walking quickly.

In April, Mohanji was coming again to see me. I welcomed him mentally by spreading jasmine flowers. While I was welcoming him, I was seeing instead of Mohanji, a bright flame of light was coming towards me, which was gradually growing in size. This vision was fixed in my eyes! Later, when I asked Mohanji about it, he said, **"Now-a-days I have become like light."**

In August 2017, Mohanji had come to our home. I went to his room. I wished to pay my respects to him by touching his feet but the doctor had told me not to bend. I sat down in front of Mohanji with his permission. Mohanji was doing some work on his mobile, and I wanted to sit down for some time near him. Suddenly, he lifted his legs from the chair and stretched them on the bed. After some time, when I got up to leave, he said, **"Come now and touch the feet."**

My happiness knew no bounds. This was no ordinary thing. I made obeisance to him repeatedly by touching his foot. Without my saying, Mohanji knew my wish and let me touch his feet. He said that, **"When anyone touches my feet with devotion, I accept their love."**

2018: In February, Mohanji came home. He was sitting having snacks in the evening. I was sitting near the dining table in front of him; suddenly the electricity went away. I had been simply gazing at him at that moment. I saw that his forehead was glowing in a beautiful gold colour. Then electricity came back and he started having his meal. I kept quiet and then Mohanji asked, **"Tayiji, what did you see?"** I replied, "I saw gold colour on your forehead." Mohanji replied, **"Yes, I am gold in colour when I am in the subtle form."**

When Mohanji came in July, he was sitting in the morning to eat *dosa* for breakfast. Before eating, he was praying as usual, offering the food to all the gods, ancestors and *Gurus*. I was sitting in front of him; Rajesh was also there. Mohanji prayed, gave a piece of *dosa* to Rajesh and said, **"Give it to Tayiji."** Then Mohanji asked me to eat. When I ate, I found that the piece of dosa was sweet. He asked, **"How is the *dosa*, Tayiji?"** "It is sweet, Mohanj," was my surprised reply. Mohanji said, **"Yes, I make food like nectar before feeding it to the deities."**

Writing the *Ashtottari* (108 names) of Mohanji

Whenever Mohanji came to our house, he would be accompanied by others who would narrate their experiences. I felt a call from inside to write the *Ashtottari* of his names and made this my resolve.

I started writing the *Ashtottari* and completed it in August 2013. When Mohanji came home, I told him that I had written his *Ashtottari*. He simply looked at me and said, **"*Ashtottari* is very good, but you did not write the name of my parents and my *gotra* (lineage)."** I was taken aback to realise he knew each line that I had written. After requesting him for the details, I included the name of his *gotra* and his parents in the *Ashtottari*.

Writing the *Sahasranama* (1000 names) of Mohanji

After writing the *Ashtottari*, I thought why not write Mohanji's *Sahasranama*? I have been listening to the experiences of so many devotees, even I myself have experienced so many. All these can come in his *Sahasranama*. When I told him this, he laughed and said that *Gurus* don't have *Sahasranama*. I said that if you are doing all the work that God does, why you cannot have *Sahasranama*. So I started writing the *Sahasranama* in August 2014.

One day, we came to know that Mohanji was staying in a nearby hotel. We went to meet Mohanji in the hotel, prostrated and sat down. Mohanji looked at me and asked, **"You are writing the *Sahasranama*, right? How many names have you written so far?"** I replied around 61 or 62. He said, **"No, you have written 74 names."** When I came home, I checked my writing and I had indeed written 74 names.

I continued my writing. In between, I could not write for two months when a baby was born in the house. Later, I restarted and completed it in December. One day, my son came home and was talking to Mohanji on the phone and said, "Today is my Tayiji's birthday, please bless her." Mohanji spoke to me and blessed me. I said, *"Guruji*, your *Sahasranama* is now completed on my birthday." He replied, **"How is this possible? It will be done on my birthday."**

When I started verifying once again, I noticed that many names were repeated two or three times; there were other mistakes. After correcting these, I kept writing more names. An instruction came to write these in English. Once the English edition was ready, we couriered it to Mohanji, and he received the *Sahasranama* in Dharamshala, exactly on his birthday.

Writing the Mohanji *Chalisa* (40 devotional couplets)

In the *Ashtottari* and *Sahasranama*, every *leela* (play) of God is translated into a name. But in the *Chalisa*, all his *leelas* are described. For example, Hanuman's deeds are described in the Hanuman *Chalisa*. In the same way, I tried to write some of Mohanji's *leelas* in his *Chalisa*. My aim was that just as Hanuman *Chalisa* is read in so many houses, if Mohanji's *Chalisa* is also read in many houses, people will know his glory.

Mohanji, an *avatar*

In all these years of connection with Mohanji, as I have explained above, he has appeared to me in many forms of God. So how can I say that he is an ordinary person? In my view, he is an avatar. An ordinary person can never take the form of Gods. Mohanji is not an ordinary person. For me, he is an avatar!

This is not just my own feeling, many *Gurus* have said so. One of them is Tyagananda Saraswati living in an ashram in Hyderabad. He said that his *Guru* gave him a *Rudraksh Mala* (rosary) and instructed him, "A *Guru* named Mohan will meet you after 15 years, give it to him." When Tyagananda Saraswati finally met Mohanji, he told Mohanji this and placed the mala in his hand. He saw the third eye on Mohanji's forehead. He also had told Mohanji, "You cannot have one Gayatri *Mantra* (sacred chant), there should be many Gayatri Mantras. You are not a regular saint. All the gods and goddesses dwell in you."

Once, Mohanji stayed in Delhi with a Guruji Maharaj for 2 days. And when Mohanji was about to leave, the Guruji Maharaj also started going with him. Mohanji said, "I am an ordinary person, why are you coming with me?" He replied, "You are not an ordinary person, you are a great man. Three generations ago, our *Guru* wrote the names of soon-to-arrive great men. Your name was amongst them."

Another time, Mohanji and his father met a young man in Kerala from the Naga community. The young man showed him a Shivling and said "This is a fire Shivling, can you take it?" Mohanji extended his hand and said, **"I can take it."** The young man warned, "It is fire, no ordinary person can lift it, only one who is of *Shivansh* (Shiva in nature) can take it. If ordinary people touch it, they will be paralyzed."

Mohanji took the Shivling in his hand. Seeing this, the young man told Mohanji, "You are not an ordinary person; you are the form of Shiva. You are

Shiva." Saying this, the man prostrated at Mohanji's feet. The man asked Mohanji's father, "Immediately upon birth, did Mohanji laugh or cry?" Mohanji's father replied that Mohanji had laughed. The man said, "Your son is not an ordinary man, he is an avatar. Let him do what he wants."

In South India, there is a type of astrology called Nadi astrology. It gives details of our previous births, based on the pulse of an individual. A Nadi astrologer said that Mohanji had not been interested in incarnating. But thanks to the prayers of mankind and some yogis, he had to incarnate and come to Earth. Mohanji will stay for 1008 years. His glory will travel the whole world, teaching the eternal religion (*Sanatana Dharma*). Finally, he will reside in India until the age of 75 giving salvation to mankind.

We are all so blessed to have taken birth at a time when an avatar has come in the form of Mohanji. Being with him, receiving the nectar of his grace, we are getting liberated.

My *koti pranaams* at the feet of my Lord Rama, Lord Krishna, Lord Shiva, Lord Datta, Lord Hanuman, and my *Guru* Brahmarishi Rajyogi Mohanji.

Painting by Marko Milovic

GOODNIGHT PAPA MOHANJI

Bavani Anop, New Zealand
December 2017

Goodnight sleep tight Oh my beloved papa
Take care of yourself know that I am thinking of you always
My dreams have become you
My thoughts have become you
Your consciousness resonates within my heart
My heart sings to you the melody of the soul's journey
To go back to the abode of the beloved
You are the sun that rises in the morning and sets in the evening
When I look into the sky I think of you
Every movement of the creation resembles your love
You are the example I want to become one day

Day and night my memories of you have become pictures in my heart
Your voice has become the sound waves in my mind
Know that the whole world loves you My lord for you are the alpha and omega
We worship you oh beloved Master

No one can compare this precious priceless love that you bestow on us

Your grace is so sweet incomparable is this taste
Oh beloved papa, no earthly language can depict
The humility and compassion of a perfect living saint
The world owes you the debt of our gratitude

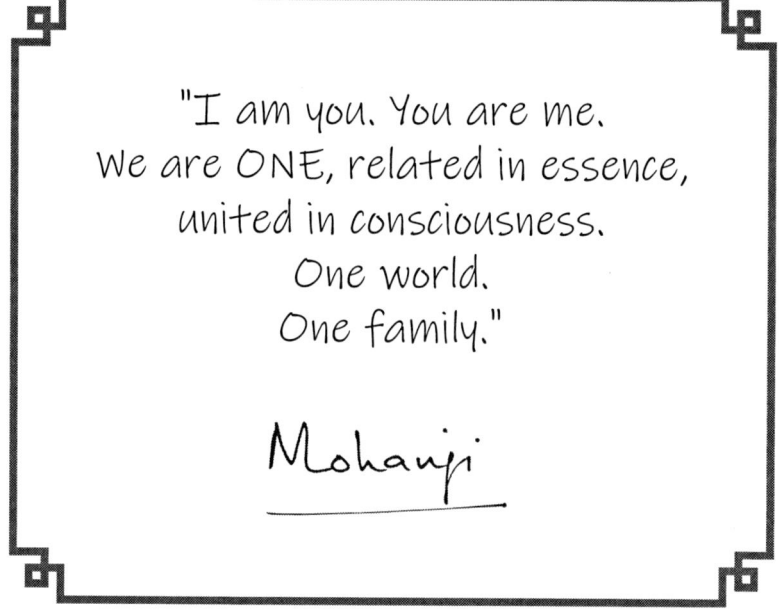

"I am you. You are me.
We are ONE, related in essence,
united in consciousness.
One world.
One family."

Mohanji

Mohanji & Biljana Vozarevic

GURU'S GIFTS

Biljana Vozarevic, Serbia

August 2018

You did not come to us for yourself, but for ourselves
So that you re-establish the pattern of every goodness
Lighting up the mind, heart and life of a ripened soul
Therefore we must not make concessions to the foul

You are filling us up with hidden power of your essence
That power becomes our inalienable heritage in a sense
We become closer and co-live with you as the Holy Spirit
How much you grant our soul is beyond our mind's limit

How many gifts which you shower upon me can I take?
As many gifts, as much emptiness in myself I can make
I am nullifying myself, accepting events with humility
In order that I can increase receptivity and eligibility

On this no-nonsense path, the path of pathlessness
You lead me accurately to higher levels of awareness
Unfaltering faith has been tested many times so far
How strong my connection is to you as my lodestar

I concentrate on you in my heart, dedicate life to bliss
I know that I am complete, there is nothing that I miss
I follow you like a shadow feeling some inner shifts
As only when I do not exist can I take your true gifts

Guru's Gifts

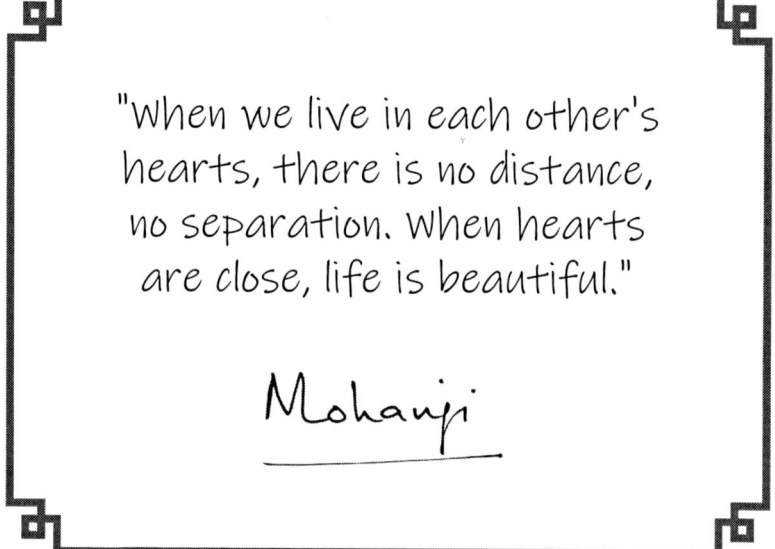

"When we live in each other's hearts, there is no distance, no separation. When hearts are close, life is beautiful."

Mohanji

Mohanji & George Obengduro

I THINK MOHANJI IS SECRETLY MY PA

George Obeng-Duro, USA

I go about busily packing his bags for his travels
While he goes about uncluttering the spaces within my being
Slowly emptying me out of all conditions and concepts
Only to fill me up with his very essence
I think Mohanji is secretly my PA.

I haul his luggage from airport to airport
Country to country, city to city
While all along he has been quietly carrying my karmic baggage
From life time to life time, eternity to eternity
Showing no signs of tiredness or stress
I think Mohanji is secretly my PA.

I stand on guard outside his room
Ensuring nobody comes to disturb him
Only to fall asleep in deep slumber
But, he's ever wakeful, always watching
He man's his post dutifully
Making sure that I never fall into the clutches of the unawakened self
I think Mohanji is secretly my PA.

Guru Leela - Mohanji and I

I hardly remember what he says
He's always the one to remind me of what I'm supposed to be doing
He's so damn good at his job
His attention to details is unmatched
He curates every minute aspect of my life's experiences
Which only seems to lead to my highest potential and evolution

He brings in the right people to love me
People to guide me and even the right people to scold me
If there are any errs in my ways
I think Mohanji is secretly my PA
Don't tell him I know his secret now.

"Nothing lasts forever. Enjoy this moment with extreme humility and gratitude. Life is irreversible. Life is happening this moment and does not wait at all for anyone or anything."

Mohanji

Mohanji & Preethi Gopalarathnam

THE MAN I KNOW OF

Preethi Gopalarathnam, India

June 2019

There is a man I know of
Who works tirelessly every moment
He gives all he has, and then some more
Touches many a heart which is open
Is he a reality, the mind questions
But there is no mistaking his actions!

There is a man I know of
Who empowers all those who look to him
Often with his own flesh and blood
With no thought of its effect on his own resources
How is he made this way, I often wonder
Because there is no logic to his generosity!

There is a man I know of
Who shines bright like a thundering lighthouse
Without a care for the fate of his safety
Just so he can guide the tossing ships
Lost in the darkness of the stormy seas called life!

There is a man I know of
My heart swells up when I think of his nature
I feel sad and happy at the same time
For I know he will go unnoticed by many
Until, all we have is his legends!

Guru Leela - Mohanji and I

There is a man I know of
And I am honoured to have met him in person
For time can do what it wants with him
But I know I will find him forever
In the deepest corner of myself.

"When devotion overflows, the devotee melts. God reciprocates and melts too. When both the devotee and the deity melt, duality disappears. God and the devotee becomes one. Overwhelming silence results. Silence becomes the state. The sound of silence is overwhelming bliss. Perfect oneness in consciousness is the aim of all beings."

Mohanji

Mohanji & Ulla Bernholdt

GRATITUDE

Ulla Bernholdt, Denmark
April 2020

Gratitude lies within every breath
connecting me to this Earth and to experience
as a gift from my lineage

Gratitude to the space between breaths
however brief the moment
I expand through universes and beyond
connecting to my Guru

Gratitude to no breath at all
here even subtle seems gross
I really acknowledge the ordeal of Masters
who incarnate
as an echo of that Silence
You will find no greater love

GLOSSARY

Aarati Religious worhhip with a light/flame

Aatma nivedanam Offering oneself to God

Acharya Teacher

Adi Guru First Guru or spiritual teacher

Aditya Hridayam Hymn dedictaed to the Sun God

Ahimsa Non-violence

Amma Mother

Appa Father

Archanam Worshipping God

Ashram Spiritual monastery

Ashtothram/Ashtottari 108 names of God

Avadhoota A complete renunciate

Avatar Incarnation

Baba/Babaji Benevolent Father

Bhajan Devotional song

Bhakti Yoga The path of devotion

Bhumi Puja Ritual performed in honour of Mother Earth

Brahma Muhurtha Ausicious time bertwen 3 am and 6 am

Glossary

Chalisa Forty verses of devotion

Charitra Character

Daasyam Being God's servant

Darshan Auspicious sight of a holy person/Deity

Devi Kavach Seeking protection through a chant invoking the divine feminine

Didi Sister

Diksha Initiation

Diwali Indian festival of lights

Doli Palanquin

Dosas Indian pancake

Dussehra Climax of the 9 nights long celebrations of Mother Goddess

Girivalam Circumambulation of a holy mountain

Gotra Lineage

Guru Shikhar Highest peak of Mount Girnar

Guru Tatwa Divine principle

Guru/Guruji Dispeller of darkness, reverential Master

Gyana Yoga Path of knowledge

Idlis Steamed cake

Janeyu Sacred thread

Kadali-vana Plantain grove

Kailashis Pilgrims to Mount Kaialsh

Kaliyuga Last of the four eras/ages

Karma Yoga Path of service

Kartik Purnima Full moon during the Kartik month of the lunar calendar

Kavacham Armour/Protection

Kirtanam Chanting God's name

Koti Ten million

Koti Pranaams Ten million salutations

Kriya Action, deed or effort

Kriya Yoga Path of action

Kshetra Purnima/Poornima Full moon viewed at a holy place/temple

Leela Divine play

Maa Mother/Divine mother

Mahasamadhi/samadhi A state that a Master enters when he consciously decides to leave his body

Mala Garland

Mantra Sacred utterance/sound of word/words

Maya Grand illusion

Nadi Meridian

Namasmarana Chanting of God's name

Naths Nine Nath saints

Navavidha Bhakti Nine forms of devotion

Paada pankajam Lotus feet

Paada sevanam Serving God's lotus feet

Pada puja Worship of the holy feet

Padukas Sacred footprints of the Master

Panch tattva Five aspects of God or absolute truth

Papad Indian thin crispy flatbread

Parikrama Circumambulation

Pranaams Salutations

Prasad Devotional offering made to God

Puja Worship

Punya Merit

Qawwali Sufi devotional music

Roti Indian flatbread

Rudraksha Seed used as prayer bead in Hinduism

Saakhyam Befriending God

Saburi Patience

Sadhana Spiritual practices

Sahasranama/Sahasranamam A thousand names of God

Sambhashan Conversation with the Divine

Sanatana Dharma Eternal way of life

Satguru A true Master

Satsang Spiritual discourse

Shakti Divine feminine

Shaktipat Transmission of universal energy by a Master

Shishya Disciple

Shivansh Shiva in nature

Shraddha Faith

Shravanam Hearing about God

Siddhas Perfected Masters

Sloka Sanskrit verse

Smaranam Remembering God

Sookshma Subtle

Sparshan Divine touch

Sri Yantra A form of mystical diagram for various Gods

Upma An Indian breakfast dish

Vandanam Prostrating to God

Vibhuti Sacred ash

Vishwaroopa Infinite form that comprises all the universes

Yagna Ritual done in front of a sacred fire

Yatra Pilgrimage

MOHANJI GAYATRI MANTRA

Om Sahasra Sooryaaya Vidmahe
Maha Aishwaryaaya Dheemahi
Tanno Mohana: Prachodayaat

I understand the essence of Mohanji as the brightness more than a thousand suns together.

I recognise this brightness as highly auspicious.

May this being called Mohanji enlighten me.